GUIDED FLIGHT DISCOVERY

PRIVATE PILOT SYLLABUS

Cover Photo
Cirrus airplane in flight courtesy of Cirrus Aircraft

ISBN 978-0-88487-654-0

Jeppesen
55 Inverness Drive East
Englewood, CO 80112-5498
Web site: www.jeppesen.com
Email: Captain@jeppesen.com
Copyright © Jeppesen
All Rights Reserved.
10001292-005   Published 1997, 2002, 2007, 2012, 2015, 2016, 2018

Preface

The *Private Pilot Syllabus* meets the requirements of 14 CFR, Part 141 and can be adapted to meet the requirements of Part 61. This syllabus refers to 14 CFR parts and regulations as Federal Aviation Regulations (FARs). The syllabus is an outline, or framework, for the course of training. Tables in Appendix B depict how the objectives and tasks listed in the ground training and flight training lessons correspond to the aeronautical knowledge and flight tasks required by Part 141, Part 61, and the FAA *Private Pilot — Airplane Airman Certification Standards (ACS)*. Instructors should refer to these tables and the pertinent sections of the regulations when teaching the course to ensure that no aeronautical knowledge areas, flight proficiency, or experience requirements are omitted during pilot training and that these requirements are documented in appropriate records and endorsements.

The syllabus has separate ground and flight training courses that are designed to be taught concurrently. The Ground Training Syllabus is divided into three stages and contains a total of 17 ground lessons. The Flight Training Syllabus also is divided into three stages and contains a total of 26 flight lessons (FLs). A stage *check* is included at the end of each stage of *flight* training, and a stage *exam* is included at the end of each stage of *ground* training. The Presolo Exam is included before the first supervised solo. In addition, End-of-Course Final Exams and an End-of-Course Flight Check are included in the syllabus prior to the conclusion of the respective ground and flight segments. The End-of-Course Flight Check is completed at the end of Stage III. The applicant must complete, or receive credit for, all of the ground and flight lessons in the *Private Pilot Syllabus*.

Computer-assisted training is incorporated into this syllabus as follows:
- The Private Pilot Online training course in the Jeppesen Learning Center
  - ◊ Ground Lessons
  - ◊ Maneuvers Lessons
- An aviation training device (ATD) for specified ground lessons

Several options to customize the syllabus to accommodate the requirements of some flight schools are described on page iv.

This syllabus offers the option of conducting the Stage I Check prior to the first solo flight. In addition, operators may choose to conduct the first solo immediately after the Stage I Check or after further dual instruction in Stage II. If operators want to incorporate either of these flight lesson sequences or utilize an aviation training device, they should check the appropriate boxes below when applying for training course outline (TCO) approval and mark the student copy of the syllabus.

❑ This syllabus has the Stage I Check (FL 10) preceding the first solo (FL 9).
❑ This syllabus has the first solo lesson (FL 9) occurring in Stage II after dual flight training on short- and soft-field takeoffs and landings (FL11) and navigation (FL14 and FL15). This change is implemented with the local solo lessons (FL 12 and FL 13) occurring after the first solo (FL9).
❑ This syllabus utilizes an ATD in the ground training segment.

_____ is enrolled in the Private
(Name)   Pilot Certification Course.

Table of Contents

Introduction

This syllabus utilizes the building-block method of teaching in which each instructional item is presented on the basis of previously learned knowledge and skill. It guides students and instructors through a lesson sequence in which new material builds on what a student has already mastered.

The Private Pilot Course contains separate ground and flight training courses. Therefore, the course may be conducted as a combined ground and flight training program or be divided into separate components. When using the integrated sequence shown in the time allocation tables, aeronautical knowledge that is pertinent to a flight lesson is taught just before that flight.

GROUND TRAINING

Ground school is an integral part of pilot certification courses and the Ground Training Syllabus meets FAR Part 141 requirements for ground training. When coordinating the ground school with flight training, each ground lesson is conducted at the point indicated in the Allocation Tables beginning on page xvii. Ground training Stages I and II are completed during Stage I of the flight training syllabus. Ground Stage III, and the End-of-Course Final Exams "A" and "B" are completed during Stage II of flight training. This sequence enables the student to complete the aeronautical knowledge segments of the syllabus before the final stage of flight training, and encourages the student to take the FAA Private Pilot Airman Knowledge Test promptly. Appendix B identifies the specific ground lessons in which knowledge areas required by Part 141 and Part 61 are covered.

In a classroom environment, ground lessons should normally be presented in numerical order. However, to provide some flexibility for adapting to individual student needs and to the training situation, the order of the lessons may be altered with approval of the chief flight instructor. Any deviation should not disturb the course continuity or objectives. Each lesson may be presented in one classroom session, or it may be divided into two or more sessions, as necessary.

GROUND TRAINING COMPONENTS

The Guided Flight Discovery Pilot Training System provides the necessary components to train for a private pilot certificate. Students and instructors should review the following list as a guide to assemble and effectively use the course materials.

Private Pilot Syllabus—the outline of the Private Pilot course. The syllabus provides a basic framework for training in a logical sequence and assigns appropriate study material prior to each lesson.

Private Pilot Textbook/e-Book—the primary source for initial study and review. Textbook chapters are references for each ground lesson. The textbook contains complete and concise explanations of the fundamental concepts and ideas that every private pilot needs to know. The subjects are organized in a logical manner to build upon previously introduced topics. Subjects are often expanded upon through the use of Discovery Insets, which are strategically placed throughout the chapters. The Summary Checklists, Key Terms, and Questions are designed to help students review and prepare for both the knowledge and practical tests.

Private Pilot Maneuvers Manual—provides illustrated step-by-step instructions for all required flight maneuvers. As study assignments prior to specific flight lessons, maneuvers lessons save training time by preparing students to perform the maneuver and reducing the time required for preflight briefing of maneuvers. Maneuvers are numbered for ease of reference, are grouped into categories based on similar operational characteristics, and presented in the order in which they are typically introduced during training.

Private Pilot Online Course—provides academic content in ground lessons with exams and interactive maneuvers lessons in a complete ground school. Online lessons are listed as references for ground lessons in this syllabus. Lessons use a combination of audio, video and graphics to clearly explain each topic. Maneuvers lessons provide step-by-step guidance with in-cockpit video showing what the pilot sees when performing each maneuver. A Learning Management System (LMS) tracks completions and test results specific to each question to assist in identifying student strengths and weaknesses.

Jeppesen FAR/AIM—includes the current Federal Aviation Regulations (FARs) and the Aeronautical Information Manual (AIM) in one publication available in printed form or as an e-Book. The FAR/AIM includes FAR Parts 1, 3, 11, 43, 48, 61, 67, 68, 71, 73, 91, 97, 103, 105, 107, 110, 119, 135, 136, 137, 141, 142, NTSB 830, and TSRs 1552 and 1562. The AIM is a complete reproduction of the FAA publication with full-color graphics and the Pilot/Controller Glossary. The AIM contains basic flight information and ATC procedures to operate effectively in the U.S. National Airspace System.

Private Pilot Exams—provide essential testing components. Required by FAR Part 141, students take a stage exam after each stage of ground training and End-of-Course Final Exams at the completion of ground training. Prior to solo flight, students must take the Presolo Exam required by FAR Part 61.

Private Pilot Airman Knowledge Test Guide—helps students understand the learning objectives for the test questions so that they can take the FAA Private Pilot Airman Knowledge Test with confidence. The test guide contains sample knowledge test questions, with correct answers, explanations, and study references. Explanations of why the other choices are wrong are included where appropriate.

LESSON EXAMS

Each ground lesson has a brief exam at the end. Students may complete the exam online in the Jeppesen Learning Center or complete the questions in the appropriate textbook chapter. As specified in the ground lesson completion standards, the exams must be scored and the student must discuss any incorrect responses with the instructor to ensure student understanding prior to beginning the next ground lesson. When a lesson is complete, the instructor assigns the next textbook chapter and section(s) or online lesson(s) for out-of-class study.

INTRODUCTION ■ Private Pilot Course

STAGE EXAMS

At the end of each stage, the student is required to successfully complete the stage exam outlined in the syllabus before beginning the next ground training stage. The stage exam evaluates the student's understanding of the knowledge areas within a stage. Successful completion of each stage exam and a review of each incorrect response is required before the student progresses to the next stage.

END-OF-COURSE FINAL EXAMS

When all of the ground lesson assignments are complete, the student should take the End-of-Course Final Exams "A" and "B" assigned in Stage III. Following the exams, the instructor should assign the student appropriate subject areas for review. After a thorough review, the student should complete the FAA Private Pilot Airman Knowledge Test without delay.

USING AN ATD FOR GROUND TRAINING

The syllabus provides for use of an ATD for ground training. An ATD is extremely effective for introducing procedures without the distraction of having to fly the airplane. If properly integrated into the ground training program, the ATD will enhance systems knowledge and procedural understanding before the student trains in the airplane.

In addition to skill enhancement, the introduction of maneuvers and procedures by instrument reference in the ATD has other advantages for both student and instructor. These include fewer distractions, more versatility in lesson presentation, repositioning, freeze functions, emergency training, and the ability to control the environment of the training session and allow the student to concentrate on the areas the instructor wants to emphasize. By following the recommended sequence of the syllabus, the student will gain maximum benefit from the integration of academic training, introduction of new maneuvers and procedures in the ATD, and subsequent practice in the airplane. The following ground lessons are particularly suited to the use of an ATD.

Ground Lesson 1 — Discovering Aviation	(1 Hour)
Ground Lesson 2 — Airplane Systems	(1 Hour)
Ground Lesson 5 — Communication and Flight Information	(1 Hour)
Ground Lesson 12 — Navigation	(1 Hour)
Ground Lesson 14 — Flying Cross-Country	(1 Hour)

If the box for ATD utilization is checked in the Preface, then the ATD becomes part of the ground training segments for the approved course, and its use is required. If the box for ATD utilization is left blank, the ATD is not part of the approved course, and its use is not required. Not checking the ATD box does not preclude a ground instructor from using an ATD. An ATD may be used in ground training just like any other classroom instructional aid.

FLIGHT TRAINING

The Flight Training Syllabus also is divided into three stages, each providing an important segment of pilot training. Tables in Appendix B specify the stages and specific flight lessons in which each flight training task required by Part 141, Part 61, and the FAA *Private Pilot — Airplane Airman Certification Standards (ACS)* is introduced, reviewed, and evaluated.

Each stage builds on previous learning and should be completed in sequence. However, to provide flexibility for adapting to individual student needs and the training environment, the syllabus lesson sequence may be altered with approval of the chief flight instructor. Any deviation should not disturb the course continuity or objectives. The Preface also includes two options for adjusting the lesson sequence to allow the first solo to occur in Stage II of flight training. If either box is checked, then the optional sequence is required for flight training.

STAGE I

In Stage I, the student develops the knowledge, skill, and habits necessary for safe solo flight. The basic maneuvers are introduced, practiced, and reviewed. In addition, the student practices airport operations, normal and crosswind takeoffs and landings, emergency procedures, and ground reference maneuvers. FAR 61.87 specifies the solo requirements for student pilots including the aeronautical knowledge that must be tested by the Presolo Exam and the maneuvers and procedures required for presolo training.

NOTE: The student must complete the Presolo Exam and Briefing prior to the first solo flight, regardless of whether that flight occurs at the end of Stage I or in Stage II.

STAGE II

This stage introduces short- and soft-field takeoffs, climbs, approaches, and landings; VOR, GPS, and ADF navigation (based on aircraft equipment); and night flying. The maneuvers introduced during this stage incorporate the skills developed during Stage I, and provide important skills necessary for the cross-country operations later in this stage.

The cross-country portion of this stage provides the information, knowledge, and skills that enable the student to begin cross-country operations. With the knowledge acquired during Stage II, the student should be able to safely conduct solo cross-country flights. Proficiency in advanced maneuvers and cross-country procedures will be evaluated during the Stage II Check.

STAGE III

The flights of Stage III are designed to provide the student with the proficiency required for the private pilot practical test. These flights are devoted to gaining experience and confidence in cross-country operations and reviewing all maneuvers within the syllabus to attain maximum pilot proficiency. Student proficiency and knowledge will be assessed by the chief instructor, assistant chief instructor, or check instructor during the Stage III Check. The student can pursue further review and instruction as necessary, in preparation for the End-of-Course Flight Check.

INTRODUCTION ■ Private Pilot Course

PREFLIGHT DISCUSSION

Prior to each dual and solo flight, the instructor should provide the student with a thorough briefing of the tasks to be covered during the lesson. The instructor should define unfamiliar terms, explain the maneuvers and objectives of each lesson, and discuss single-pilot resource management (SRM) concepts related to each lesson. The Preflight Discussion should be tailored to the specific flight, the local environment, and especially to the needs of the student.

AIRPLANE PRACTICE

Each flight should begin with a review of previously-learned maneuvers before any new maneuvers are introduced. To ensure that students efficiently utilize solo flight training lessons, the instructor should train the student in the maneuvers to be performed during the flight and discuss what is expected to be accomplished during that lesson.

FSS, FTD, OR ATD

The syllabus allows for instruction in a flight simulation training device (FSTD), which is defined as a full flight simulator (FSS) or flight training device (FTD). Training in an FSS that meets the requirements of 141.41(a) may be credited for a maximum of 20 percent of the total flight training hour requirements (20%× 35 hours = 7.0 hours). Training in an FTD that meets the requirements of 141.41(b) may be credited for a maximum of 15 percent of the total flight training hour requirements (15% × 35 hours = 5.25 hours). Training in an FSS or FTD, if used in combination, may be credited for a maximum of 20 percent of the total flight training hour requirements However, credit for training in an FTD cannot exceed 15 percent.

The regulations do not specifically address the use of an ATD to meet private pilot flight training requirements. However, according to FAR 61.4(c), the FAA may approve a device other than an FSS or FTD for specific purposes. An ATD may be used for flight training credit if the school obtains an FAA letter of authorization (LOA). AC 61-136A — *FAA Approval of Aviation Training Devices and Their Use for Training and Experience* provides guidelines for schools to obtain an LOA that approves an ATD for meeting up to 15% of the total flight training requirements.

POSTFLIGHT DEBRIEFING

The Postflight Debriefing is as important as the Preflight Discussion. The student should perform a self-critique of maneuvers/procedures and SRM skills. This *learner-centered grading* is especially helpful in developing decision-making skills. If the student is having trouble mastering a skill, both the student and instructor should plan for improving performance. An effective Postflight Briefing increases retention and helps the student prepare for the next lesson. As a guide, a minimum of 1/2 hour per flight is recommended for the Preflight Discussion and Postflight Briefing combined.

STUDENT STAGE CHECKS

Stage checks measure the student's accomplishments during each stage of training. The conduct of each stage check is the responsibility of the chief instructor. However, the chief instructor may delegate authority for conducting stage checks and the End-of-Course Flight Check to the assistant chief instructor or a designated check instructor. This procedure provides close supervision of training and provides another opinion on the student's progress. The stage check also helps the chief instructor check the effectiveness of the instructors.

An examination of the building-block theory of learning will show that it is extremely important for progress and proficiency to be satisfactory before the student enters a new stage of training. Therefore, the next stage should not begin until the student successfully completes the stage check. Failure to follow this progression might defeat the purpose of the stage check and degrade the overall effectiveness of the course.

PILOT BRIEFINGS
The following three pilot briefings are assigned in the flight syllabus.
1. Presolo Exam and Briefing
2. Solo Cross-Country Briefing
3. Private Pilot Practical Test Briefing

Pilot briefings are contained in Appendix A of this syllabus. Each briefing consists of a series of questions to prepare the student for the knowledge and tasks required in subsequent solo lessons and the practical test. The student should review the appropriate briefing questions in advance and research the answers to gain optimum benefit from the briefing.

The briefings should be conducted as private tutoring sessions to test each student's comprehension. Hold the briefings in a comfortable classroom or office environment, and schedule ample time. Discuss every question thoroughly to ensure the student understands the key points. Correct placement of the briefings is indicated in the Allocation Tables

The Presolo Exam and Briefing is unique. As specified in FAR 61.87, the student must demonstrate satisfactory knowledge of the required subject areas by completing a knowledge exam. This exam is to be administered and graded by the instructor who endorses the student pilot certificate for solo flight and must include questions on applicable portions of FAR Parts 61 and 91. In addition, instructors should modify the exam as necessary to make it appropriate for the aircraft to be flown and the local flying environment.

PART 61 OPERATION
The *Private Pilot Syllabus* is designed to meet all the requirements of Part 141, Appendix B. It can be adapted to meet the flight time (airplane, single-engine) requirements of FAR 61.109. The basic difference between the flight time requirements of Part 141 and Part 61 is that under Part 61, the student must have at least 40 hours of flight time that includes at least 20 hours of flight instruction from an authorized instructor and 10 hours of solo flight training (in specified areas of operation). The flight time requirements of Part 141 are nearly the same, except total flight time is only 35 hours. Adapting this syllabus to Part 61 training requires only a slight modification of individual flight lesson times.

The ground training requirements under Part 61 specify that an applicant for a knowledge test must have a logbook endorsement from an authorized instructor

INTRODUCTION ■ Private Pilot Course

who conducted the training or reviewed the applicant's home study course. The endorsement must indicate satisfactory completion of the ground instruction or home study course required for the certificate or rating being sought. A home study course for the purposes of Part 61 is a course of study in those aeronautical knowledge areas specified in FAR 61.105, and organized by a pilot school, publisher, flight or ground instructor, or by the student. The Jeppesen Private Pilot Course satisfies this requirement. As a practical consideration, students seeking pilot certification under Part 61 should receive some formal ground training, either in the classroom or from an authorized flight or ground instructor.

CREDIT FOR PREVIOUS TRAINING

According to FAR 141.77, when a student transfers from one FAA-approved school to another approved school, course credits obtained in the previous course of training may be credited for 50 percent of the curriculum requirements by the receiving school. However, the receiving school must determine the amount of credit to be allowed based upon a proficiency test or knowledge test, or both, conducted by the receiving school. A student who enrolls in a course of training may receive credit for 25 percent of the curriculum requirements for knowledge and experience gained in a non-Part 141 flight school, and the credit must be based upon a proficiency test or knowledge test, or both, conducted by the receiving school. The amount of credit for previous training allowed, whether received from an FAA-approved school or other source, is determined by the receiving school. In addition, the previous provider of the training must certify the kind and amount of training given, and the result of each stage check and end-of-course test, if applicable.

Course Overview

The Private Pilot Course is designed to coordinate the academic study assignments and flight training required to operate in an increasingly complex aviation environment. New subject matter is introduced and evaluated during the ground lessons using the following methods, as chosen by your school.

1. In-depth textbook assignments with study questions:
   ◊ *Private Pilot* textbook/e-Book
   ◊ *Private Pilot Maneuvers* manual/e-Book
2. The Private Pilot online course in the Jeppesen Learning Center
3. Instructor/student discussions
4. Stage exams and end-of-course exams

For best results, students should complete ground lessons just prior to the respective flight lessons, as outlined in the syllabus. However, it is also acceptable to present lessons in a formal ground school before introducing the student to the airplane. If significant time has elapsed between the ground lesson and the associated flight, the instructor should conduct a short review of essential material. Generally, flight lessons should not be conducted until the student has completed the prerequisite ground lessons.

In selected flight lessons, the abbreviation "VR" indicates that students should maintain aircraft control by using outside visual references. "IR" indicates that they should use instrument references. No indication of either "VR" or "IR," means that normal private pilot maneuvers or procedures should be conducted by outside visual references.

THE PRIVATE PILOT CERTIFICATION COURSE AIRPLANE SINGLE-ENGINE LAND

COURSE OBJECTIVES
The student will obtain the knowledge, skill, and aeronautical experience necessary to meet the requirements for a private pilot certificate with an airplane category rating and a single-engine land class rating.

COURSE COMPLETION STANDARDS
The student must demonstrate through knowledge exams and flight checks, and show through appropriate records that he/she meets the knowledge, skill, and experience requirements necessary to obtain a private pilot certificate with an airplane category rating and a single-engine land class rating.

OVERVIEW ■ Private Pilot Course

STUDENT INFORMATION

COURSE ENROLLMENT
There are no prerequisites for initial enrollment in the ground portion of the Private Pilot course.

REQUIREMENTS FOR SOLO FLIGHT
Before you may fly solo, you must hold a recreational, sport, or student pilot certificate and at least a current third-class medical certificate. You must be at least 16 years of age to obtain a student pilot certificate and be able to read, speak, write, and understand the English language. Remember that solo flight operations require specific training, successful completion of a presolo knowledge exam, and endorsements from your flight instructor.

REQUIREMENTS FOR GRADUATION
To graduate, you must be at least 17 years of age, be able to read, speak, write, and understand the English language, meet the time requirements listed in the Allocation Tables, and satisfactorily complete the training outlined in this syllabus. When you meet the minimum requirements of Part 141, Appendix B, you are eligible for graduation.

LESSON DESCRIPTION AND STAGES OF TRAINING
This syllabus describes each lesson, including the objectives, references, topics, and completion standards. The stage objectives and standards are described at the beginning of each stage within the syllabus.

FLIGHT CHECKS AND GROUND EXAMS
The syllabus incorporates stage checks and the End-of-Course Flight Check as required by Part 141, Appendix B. The chief instructor is responsible for ensuring that each student accomplishes the required stage checks and the End-of-Course Flight Check in accordance with the school's approved training course. However, the chief instructor may delegate authority for stage checks and the End-of-Course Flight Check to the assistant chief or check instructor. You also must complete the academic knowledge tests—stage exams, pilot briefings, and End-of-Course Final Exams—that are described within the syllabus.

OVERVIEW ■ Private Pilot Course

Ground Training Overview

Completion of this course is based solely upon compliance with the minimum requirements of FAR Part 141. The accompanying tables with times shown in hours are provided mainly for guidance in achieving regulatory compliance.

PRIVATE PILOT CERTIFICATION COURSE
AIRPLANE SINGLE-ENGINE LAND

	GROUND TRAINING					
	Maneuvers Class Discussion and Online Training	ATD	Ground Lessons	Pilot Briefings	Stage/Final Exams	Exam Debriefings
GROUND STAGE I	3.0	3.0	10.0		1.0	As Required
GROUND STAGE II	3.0		6.0	2.0	1.0	As Required
GROUND STAGE III	3.0	2.0	8.0	2.0	4.0	1.0
TOTALS	9.0	5.0	24.0	4.0	6.0	1.0

NOTE: 1. The first column shows the recommended *Private Pilot Maneuvers* class discussion and/or online training time.
2. The second column shows maximum ATD time when an ATD is approved for the course.
3. The third column shows the minimum recommended training time for ground lessons, which may include class discussion or online lessons. Times shown in columns 1 and 2 may be credited toward the total time shown in column 3 as follows:
   • Up to 9 hours of *Private Pilot Maneuvers* class discussion and/or online training.
   • Up to 5 hours of ATD training.
   To recieve credit for ATD training time, the associated course approval must be obtained. (See Preface.)

Flight Training Overview

PRIVATE PILOT CERTIFICATION COURSE
AIRPLANE SINGLE-ENGINE LAND

	FLIGHT TRAINING							
	DUAL					SOLO		
	Day Local	Day Cross Country	Night Local	Night Cross Country	Instrument	Day Local	Cross Country	Dual/Solo Combined Totals
FLIGHT STAGE I	9.0 (8.5)				(1.0)	.5 (0)		9.5 (8.5)
FLIGHT STAGE II	4.0 (4.5)	2.0	1.0	2.0	(2.0)	2.0 (2.5)	2.5	13.5 (14.5)
FLIGHT STAGE III	6.0						6.0	12.0
TOTALS	19.0	2.0	1.0	2.0	(3.0)	2.5	8.5	35.0

NOTE: 1. The Presolo Exam, Briefing, and Flight Lesson 9 can be moved to Flight Stage II if the Stage Check precedes the first solo. The numbers in parentheses indicate the stage times if the Stage I Check precedes the first solo.

2. Dual instrument training in the airplane is allocated to portions of flight lessons 3, 4, 5, 7, 8, 14, 15, 17, and 18 for a total of 3.0 hours. The minimum recommended times are .2 hours (12 minutes) each for Flight Lesson 3, 4, 5, 7, and 8 and .5 hours (30 minutes) each for Flight Lessons 14, 15, 17, and 18. The total of 3.0 hours of instrument training is specified in Part 141, Appendix B.

3. For the purpose of meeting cross-country time requirements for a private pilot certificate, a landing must be accomplished at a straight-line distance of more than 50 nautical miles from the original point of departure.

Private Pilot Syllabus

Allocation Tables

LESSON TIME ALLOCATION

Maneuvers Class Discussion and Online Training	ATD	Ground Lessons	Pilot Briefings	Stage/Final Exams	Exam Debriefings		Day Local	Day Cross-Country	Night Local	Night Cross-Country	Instrument	Day Local	Cross-Country
						Ground Training / **Flight Training — Dual / Solo**							

GROUND STAGE I, II AND FLIGHT STAGE I

Maneuvers	ATD	Ground Lessons	Pilot Briefings	Stage/Final Exams	Exam Debriefings	Lesson	Day Local	Day Cross-Country	Night Local	Night Cross-Country	Instrument	Day Local (Solo)	Cross-Country (Solo)
	1.0	2.0				GL 1 – Discovering Aviation							
	1.0	2.0				GL 2 – Airplane Systems							
						FL 1 – Ground Operations / Basic Maneuvers	.5						
		2.0				GL 3 – Aerodynamic Principles							
1.0						FL 2 – Ground Operations / Basic Maneuvers	1.0						
		2.0				GL 4 – The Flight Environment							
1.0						FL 3 – Slow Flight / Stalls / Basic Instrument	1.0				(.2)		
	1.0	2.0				GL 5 – Communication and Flight Information							
1.0						FL 4 – Emergency Procedures / Steep Turns	1.0				(.2)		
				1.0	As Req.	GL 6 – Stage I Exam							
1.0						FL 5 – Ground Reference Maneuvers	1.0				(.2)		
		2.0				GL 7 – Meteorology for Pilots							
1.0						FL 6 – Takeoffs, Landings, and Go-Arounds	1.0						
		2.0				GL 8 – Federal Aviation Regulations							
1.0						FL 7 – Review	1.0				(.2)		
		2.0				GL 9 – Interpreting Weather Data							
			2.0		As Req.	Presolo Exam and Briefing							
						FL 8 – Review	1.0				(.2)		
						FL 9 – First Solo	.5					.5	
				1.0	As Req.	GL 10 – Stage II Exam							
						FL 10 – Stage I Check	1.0						
6.0	3.0	16.0	2.0	2.0	As Req.	**Ground Stage Totals**	9.0 (8.5)				(1.0)	.5 (0)	

NOTE:
1. The first column shows the recommended *Private Pilot Maneuvers* discussion and/or online training time.
2. The second column shows maximum ATD time when an ATD is approved for the course.
3. The third column shows the minimum recommended training time for ground lessons, which may include class discussion or online lessons. Times shown in columns 1 and 2 may be credited toward the total time shown in column 3 for the Private Pilot Course as follows:
   - Up to 9 hours of *Private Pilot Maneuvers* class discussion and/or online training.
   - Up to 5 hours of ATD training.
   To recieve credit for ATD training time, the associated course approval must be obtained. (See Preface.)
4. Check the applicable boxes in the Preface to select the following course options. Course approval must be obtained to:
   - Receive credit for ATD training time.
   - Complete the Stage I Check prior to the first solo.
   - Complete Flight Lessons 11, 14, and 15 prior to the first solo.
5. The numbers in parentheses for Dual and Solo Day Local flight times represent total stage times if the Stage 1 check precedes the first solo.

OVERVIEW ■ Private Pilot Course

OVERVIEW ■ Private Pilot Course

LESSON TIME ALLOCATION

Maneuvers Class Discussion and Online Training	ATD	Ground Lessons	Pilot Briefings	Stage/Final Exams	Exam Debriefings		Dual Day Local	Dual Day Cross-Country	Dual Night Local	Dual Night Cross-Country	Dual Instrument	Solo Day Local	Solo Cross-Country
						GROUND STAGE III AND FLIGHT STAGE II							
		2.0				GL 11 – Airplane Performance							
1.0						FL 11 – Short/Soft-Field Takeoffs and Landings	1.0						
	1.0	2.0				GL 12 – Navigation							
						FL 12 – Solo Local						1.0	
		2.0				GL 13 – Human Factor Principles							
						FL 13 – Solo Local						1.0	
	1.0	2.0				GL 14 – Flying Cross Country							
1.0						FL 14 – Navigation	1.0				(.5)		
				1.0	As Req.	GL 15 – Stage III Exam							
						FL 15 – Navigation Review	1.0				(.5)		
						FL 16 – Night Local			1.0				
1.0						FL 17 – Dual Cross-Country		2.0			(.5)		
						FL 18 – Night Cross-Country				2.0	(.5)		
			2.0			Solo Cross-Country Briefing							
						FL 19 – Solo Cross-Country							2.5
				3.0	1.0	GL 16 & 17 – Final Exams A & B							
						FL 20 – Stage II Check	1.0						
3.0	2.0	8.0	2.0	4.0	1.0	**Stage Totals**	4.0 (4.5)	2.0	1.0	2.0	(2.0)	2.0 (2.5)	2.5

NOTE:

1. The first column shows the recommended *Private Pilot Maneuvers* discussion and/or online training time.

2. The second column shows maximum ATD time when an ATD is approved for the course.

3. The third column shows the minimum recommended training time for ground lessons, which may include class discussion or online lessons. Times shown in columns 1 and 2 may be credited toward the total time shown in column 3 for the Private Pilot Course as follows:
   - Up to 9 hours of *Private Pilot Maneuvers* class discussion and/or online training.
   - Up to 5 hours of ATD training.
   To recieve credit for ATD training time, the associated course approval must be obtained. (See Preface.)

4. Check the applicable boxes in the Preface to select the following course options. Course approval must be obtained to:
   - Receive credit for ATD training time.
   - Complete the Stage I Check prior to the first solo.
   - Complete Flight Lessons 11, 14, and 15 prior to the first solo.

5. The numbers in parentheses for Dual and Solo Day Local flight times represent total stage times if the Stage 1 check precedes the first solo.

LESSON TIME ALLOCATION

Maneuvers Class Discussion and Online Training	ATD	Ground Lessons	Pilot Briefings	Stage/Final Exams	Exam Debriefings	Ground Training / Flight Stage	Day Local	Day Cross-Country	Night Local	Night Cross-Country	Instrument	Day Local (Solo)	Cross-Country (Solo)
						FLIGHT STAGE III							
						FL 21 – Solo Cross-Country							2.0
						FL 22 – Solo Cross-Country							4.0
						FL 23 – Practical Test Preparation	2.0				As Req.		
						FL 24 – Practical Test Preparation	2.0				As Req.		
						FL 25 – Stage III Check	1.0						
			As Req.			Private Pilot Practical Test Briefing							
						FL 26 – End-of-Course Flight Check	1.0				As Req.		
						Stage Totals	6.0						6.0
9.0	5.0	24.0	4.0	6.0	1.0	Private Pilot Course – Overall Totals	19.0	2.0	1.0	2.0	(3.0)	2.5	8.5

The individual times shown on the accompanying Lesson Time Allocation tables are for instructor/student guidance only; they are not mandatory for each ground lesson, flight lesson, or stage of training. At the conclusion of this course, the student must meet the minimum requirements of FAR Part 141, Appendix B, for each catagory in order to graduate. Preflight and postflight briefing times are not specified, but a minimum of .5 hours for each dual and solo flight is suggested. The times for Pilot Briefings, although assigned and completed along with selected flight lessons, are considered part of ground training.

OVERVIEW ■ Private Pilot Course

OVERVIEW ■ **Private Pilot Course**

Private Pilot Ground Training Syllabus

GROUND TRAINING COURSE OBJECTIVES

The student will obtain the aeronautical knowledge required by FAR Part 141 and Part 61 for private pilot certification and meet the prerequisites in Part 61 for the FAA Private Pilot Airman Knowledge Test.

GROUND TRAINING COURSE COMPLETION STANDARDS

Through knowledge exams and records, the student must demonstrate the aeronautical knowledge required by FAR Part 141 and Part 61 for private pilot certification. The student must also demonstrate the knowledge necessary to pass the FAA Private Pilot Airman Knowledge Test and show that the prerequisites specified in Part 61 have been met.

Stage I

STAGE OBJECTIVES

During this stage, the student is introduced to pilot training, aviation opportunities, and human factors in aviation, and explores airplane systems and aerodynamic principles. The student also learns about the safety of flight, operating at airports, interpreting aeronautical charts, and airspace requirements. In addition, the student gains knowledge about ATC services, radio procedures and how to locate and use sources of flight information.

STAGE COMPLETION STANDARDS

The student must pass the Stage I Exam with a minimum score of 80 percent, and review each incorrect response with the instructor to ensure complete understanding before starting Stage II.

STAGE I ■ Ground Training Syllabus

GROUND LESSON 1

REFERENCES

NOTE: Students should study the listed references prior to beginning the Ground Lesson 1 instructional session.

Private Pilot Textbook/e-Book
Chapter 1 — Discovering Aviation (Sections A, B, C)

Private Pilot Online — Jeppesen Learning Center
Module 1 — Discovering Aviation (GL 1, 2, 3)

OBJECTIVES

• Recognize the essential components of the school's pilot training program.
Part 141/61 Aeronautical Knowledge
• Applicable Federal Aviation Regulations for private pilot privileges, limitations, and flight operations:
  ◊ Identify the medical and currency requirements for piloting an airplane.
  ◊ Recognize the requirements to act as pilot in command of different types of aircraft.
• Aeronautical decision making and judgment:
  ◊ Identify the concepts that apply to single-pilot resource management.
  ◊ Explain how to perform a self-assessment prior to flight and briefings during flight operations.
  ◊ Recognize physiological factors that affect your performance during flight.

CONTENT

COURSE OVERVIEW
❑ Course Components
❑ Exams and Tests
❑ Policies and Procedures
❑ Student/Instructor Expectations
❑ Use of a Full Flight Simulators (FSS), Flight Training Devices (FTD), and/or Aviation Training Device (ATD)

SECTION A — PILOT TRAINING
GL 2 ONLINE — PILOT TRAINING FAQS
❑ Federal Aviation Administration
❑ Private Pilot Requirements
❑ Medical Certificates and BasicMed
❑ Ground and Flight Training Process
❑ Private Pilot Privileges and Limitations
❑ Aircraft Category and Class

SECTION B — AVIATION OPPORTUNITIES
GL 1 ONLINE — AVIATION OPPORTUNITIES
❑ New Aviation Experiences
❑ Aviation Organizations
❑ Category and Class Ratings
❑ Additional Pilot Certificates
❑ Aviation Careers

SECTION C — INTRODUCTION TO HUMAN FACTORS
GL 3 ONLINE — INTRODUCTION TO HUMAN FACTORS
❑ Single-Pilot Resource Management
  ◊ Aeronautical Decision Making and Judgment
  ◊ Risk Management
  ◊ Task Management
  ◊ Situational Awareness
  ◊ Controlled Flight into Terrain (CFIT) Awareness
  ◊ Automation Management
❑ Aviation Physiology
  ◊ Pressure Effects
  ◊ Motion Sickness
  ◊ Fatigue and Noise
  ◊ Alcohol, Drugs, and Performance

COMPLETION STANDARDS:
- Demonstrate understanding of policies and procedures that apply to the school's pilot training program.
- Demonstrate understanding of pilot training programs, opportunities in aviation, and human factors during oral quizzing by the instructor.
- Complete with a minimum score of 80 percent: questions for Chapter 1A, 1B, and 1C; or online exams for GL 2 and 3. With the instructor, review each incorrect response to ensure complete understanding before starting Ground Lesson 2.

STUDY ASSIGNMENT

Private Pilot Textbook/e-Book
Chapter 2 — Airplane Systems (Sections A, B, C)

Private Pilot Online — Jeppesen Learning Center
Module 2 — Airplane Systems (GL 4, 5, 6)

STAGE I ■ Ground Training Syllabus

3

GROUND LESSON 2

REFERENCES

Private Pilot Textbook/e-Book
Chapter 2 — Airplane Systems (Sections A, B, C)

Private Pilot Online — Jeppesen Learning Center
Module 2 — Airplane Systems (GL 4, 5, 6)

OBJECTIVES
Part 141/61 Aeronautical Knowledge
- Applicable Federal Aviation Regulations (FARs) for private pilot privileges, limitations, and flight operations:
  ◊ Identify the inspections and aircraft logbook documentation that are required for airworthiness.
  ◊ Identify the equipment required for VFR flight under FAR 91.205 and the procedures to fly with inoperative equipment.
- Principles of powerplants and aircraft systems:
  ◊ Identify airplane components.
  ◊ Explain how aircraft engines and related systems operate.
  ◊ Describe flight instrument functions and operating characteristics, including errors and common malfunctions.

CONTENT

SECTION A — AIRPLANES
GL 4 ONLINE — AIRPLANES
- ❑ The Fuselage
- ❑ The Wing
- ❑ The Empennage
- ❑ Trim Devices
- ❑ Landing Gear
- ❑ The Powerplant
- ❑ Pilot's Operating Handbook (POH)
- ❑ Airworthiness Requirements

SECTION B — THE POWERPLANT AND RELATED SYSTEMS
GL 5 ONLINE — THE POWERPLANT AND RELATED SYSTEMS
- ❑ Reciprocating Engine Operation
- ❑ Induction Systems—Carburetor and Fuel Injection
- ❑ Supercharging and Turbocharging
- ❑ The Ignition System
- ❑ Abnormal Combustion
- ❑ Fuel Systems
- ❑ Refueling
- ❑ Oil Systems

STAGE I ■ Ground Training Syllabus

- Cooling Systems
- The Exhaust System
- Propellers—Fixed-Pitch and Constant-Speed
- Propeller Hazards
- Full Authority Digital Engine Control (FADEC)
- Electrical Systems

SECTION C — FLIGHT INSTRUMENTS
GL 6 ONLINE — FLIGHT INSTRUMENTS

- Pitot-Static Instruments
- Airspeed Indicator
- Altimeter
- Vertical Speed Indicator
- Gyroscopic Instruments
- Attitude Indicator
- Heading Indicator
- Magnetic Compass
- Integrated Flight Displays

COMPLETION STANDARDS

- Demonstrate understanding of airplane components and systems, the powerplant and related systems, and flight instruments during oral quizzing by the instructor.
- Complete with a minimum score of 80 percent: questions for Chapter 2A, 2B, and 2C or online exams for GL 4, 5, and 6. With the instructor, review each incorrect response to ensure complete understanding before starting Ground Lesson 3.

STUDY ASSIGNMENT

Private Pilot Textbook/e-Book
  Chapter 3 — Aerodynamic Principles (Sections A, B, C)

Private Pilot Online — Jeppesen Learning Center
  Module 3 — Aerodynamic Principles (GL 7, 8, 9)

GROUND LESSON 3

REFERENCES

Private Pilot Textbook/e-Book
  Chapter 3 — Aerodynamic Principles (Sections A, B, C)

Private Pilot Online — Jeppesen Learning Center
  Module 3 — Aerodynamic Principles (GL 7, 8, 9)

STAGE I ■ **Ground Training Syllabus**

OBJECTIVES

Part 141/61 Aeronautical Knowledge
- Principles of aerodynamics:
  ◊ Describe the four forces of flight.
  ◊ Explain the aerodynamic principles and design characteristics that apply to airplane stability and maneuverability.
- Stall awareness, spin entry, spins, and spin recovery techniques:
  ◊ Recognize the stall and spin characteristics related to training airplanes.
  ◊ Explain how to recognize and recover from stalls and spins.

CONTENT

SECTION A — FOUR FORCES OF FLIGHT
GL 7 ONLINE — FOUR FORCES OF FLIGHT
- ❑ Lift
- ❑ Airfoils
- ❑ Pilot Control of Lift
- ❑ Weight
- ❑ Thrust
- ❑ Drag
- ❑ Ground Effect

SECTION B — STABILITY
GL 8 ONLINE — STABILITY
- ❑ Three Axes of Flight
- ❑ Longitudinal Stability
- ❑ Center of Gravity Position
- ❑ Lateral Stability
- ❑ Directional Stability
- ❑ Stalls
- ❑ Spins
- ❑ Spin Recovery

SECTION C — AERODYNAMICS OF MANEUVERING FLIGHT
GL 9 ONLINE — AERODYNAMICS OF MANEUVERING FLIGHT
- ❑ Climbing Flight
- ❑ Left-Turning Tendencies
- ❑ Descending Flight
- ❑ Turning Flight
- ❑ Load Factor

COMPLETION STANDARDS

- Demonstrate understanding of the four forces of flight, stability, maneuverability, stalls, and spins during oral quizzing by the instructor.
- Complete with a minimum score of 80 percent: questions for Chapter 3A, 3B, and 3C; or online exams for GL 7, 8, and 9. With the instructor, review each incorrect response to ensure complete understanding before starting Ground Lesson 4.

STUDY ASSIGNMENT

Private Pilot Textbook/e-Book
Chapter 4 — The Flight Environment (Sections A, B, C, D)

Private Pilot Online — Jeppesen Learning Center
Module 4 — The Flight Environment (GL 10, 11, 12, 13)

GROUND LESSON 4

REFERENCES

Private Pilot Textbook/e-Book
Chapter 4 — The Flight Environment (Sections A, B, C, D)

Private Pilot Online — Jeppesen Learning Center
Module 4 — The Flight Environment (GL 10, 11, 12, 13)

OBJECTIVES

Part 141/61 Aeronautical Knowledge
- Safe and efficient operation of aircraft, including collision avoidance:
  ◊ Explain collision avoidance procedures, including visual scanning techniques and runway incursion avoidance.
  ◊ Recall right-of-way rules and minimum safe altitudes.
- Applicable subjects of the Aeronautical Information Manual:
  ◊ Interpret airport markings, signs, and lighting.
  ◊ Identify airspace types and operating requirements.
- Aeronautical charts for VFR navigation using pilotage, dead reckoning, and navigation systems:
  ◊ Interpret aeronautical chart symbology.
  ◊ Interpret communication and navigation information on aeronautical charts.

CONTENT

SECTION A — SAFETY OF FLIGHT
GL 10 ONLINE — SAFETY OF FLIGHT
- ❑ Collision Avoidance
- ❑ Visual Scanning
- ❑ Cockpit Traffic Displays
- ❑ Airport Operations
- ❑ Right-of-Way Rules
- ❑ Minimum Safe Altitudes
- ❑ Wire Strike Avoidance
- ❑ Flight Over Hazardous Terrain
- ❑ Taxiing in Wind
- ❑ Positive Exchange of Flight Controls

STAGE I ■ **Ground Training Syllabus**

STAGE I ■ Ground Training Syllabus

SECTION B — AIRPORTS
GL 11 ONLINE — AIRPORTS
❏ Controlled and Uncontrolled Airports
❏ Runway Layout
❏ Traffic Pattern
❏ Airport Visual Aids
❏ Runway and Taxiway Markings
❏ Ramp Area Hand Signals
❏ Runway Incursion Avoidance
❏ Land and Hold Short Operations (LAHSO)
❏ Airport Lighting
❏ Visual Glideslope Indicators
❏ Approach Light Systems
❏ Pilot-Controlled Lighting
❏ Airport Security

SECTION C — AERONAUTICAL CHARTS
GL 12 ONLINE — AERONAUTICAL CHARTS
❏ Latitude and Longitude
❏ Projections
❏ Sectional Charts
❏ VFR Terminal Area Charts
❏ Chart Symbology

SECTION D — AIRSPACE
GL 13 ONLINE — AIRSPACE
❏ Airspace Classifications
❏ Uncontrolled Airspace
❏ Controlled Airspace
  ◊ Class E
  ◊ Class D
  ◊ Class C
  ◊ Class B
  ◊ Class A
❏ Special VFR
❏ Special Use Airspace
❏ Other Airspace Areas
❏ Temporary Flight Restrictions (TFRs)
❏ Air Defense Identification Zone (ADIZ)
❏ Washington DC Special Flight Rules Area (SFRA)
❏ Intercept Procedures

COMPLETION STANDARDS
• Demonstrate understanding of collision avoidance, right-of-way rules, minimum safe altitudes, airport marking and lighting, runway incursion avoidance, LAHSO, aeronautical charts, and airspace requirements during oral quizzing by the instructor.

- Complete with a minimum score of 80 percent: questions for Chapter 4A, 4B, 4C, and 4D; or online exams for GL 10, 11, 12, and 13. With the instructor, review each incorrect response to ensure complete understanding before starting Ground Lesson 5.

STUDY ASSIGNMENT

Private Pilot Textbook/e-Book
Chapter 5 — Communication and Flight Information (Sections A, B, C)

Private Pilot Online — Jeppesen Learning Center
Module 5 — Communication and Flight Information (GL 14, 15, 16)

GROUND LESSON 5

REFERENCES

Private Pilot Textbook/e-Book
Chapter 5 — Communication and Flight Information (Sections A, B, C)

Private Pilot Online — Jeppesen Learning Center
Module 5 — Communication and Flight Information (GL 14, 15, 16)

OBJECTIVES

Part 141/61 Aeronautical Knowledge
- Applicable subjects of the Aeronautical Information Manual and the appropriate FAA advisory circulars:
  ◊ Recognize the characteristics of the ADS-B system and radar operation.
  ◊ Explain how to properly operate a transponder.
  ◊ Identify the services provided by ATC and Flight Service.
- Radio communication procedures:
  ◊ Describe the proper techniques for transmitting on the radio.
  ◊ Explain the procedures for communicating at controlled and uncontrolled airports.
- Preflight action that includes how to obtain information on runway lengths at airports of intended use and data on takeoff and landing distances:
  ◊ Recognize the sources of flight information.
  ◊ Locate flight information by using Chart Supplements, NOTAMs, FARs, the AIM, and advisory circulars.

CONTENT

SECTION A — ATC SERVICES
GL 14 ONLINE — ATC SERVICES
❑ ADS-B System
❑ Radar
❑ Transponders

- ❏ Flight Service
- ❏ Control Tower Services
- ❏ Automatic Terminal Information Service (ATIS)
- ❏ TRACON and ARTCC Services
- ❏ Interpreting Traffic Advisories

SECTION B — RADIO PROCEDURES
GL 15 ONLINE — RADIO PROCEDURES
- ❏ VHF Communication Equipment
- ❏ Using the Radio
- ❏ Phonetic Alphabet
- ❏ Using Numbers on the Radio
- ❏ Coordinated Universal Time (UTC)
- ❏ Common Traffic Advisory Frequency (CTAF)
- ❏ Controlled Airports
- ❏ ATC Facilities
- ❏ Reading Back Clearances
- ❏ Lost Communication Procedures
- ❏ Emergency Procedures and ELTs

SECTION C — SOURCES OF FLIGHT INFORMATION
GL 16 ONLINE — SOURCES OF FLIGHT INFORMATION
- ❏ Locating Flight Information
- ❏ Aeronautical Charts
- ❏ Chart Supplements
- ❏ Airport/Facility Directory
- ❏ Electronic Flight Bag (EFB)
- ❏ Notices to Airmen (NOTAMs)
- ❏ Federal Aviation Regulations (FARs)
- ❏ Aeronautical Information Manual (AIM)
- ❏ Advisory Circulars (ACs)

COMPLETION STANDARDS
- Demonstrate understanding of ATC services, radio procedures and sources of flight information during oral quizzing by the instructor.
- Complete with a minimum score of 80 percent: questions for Chapter 5A, 5B, and 5C; or online exams for GL 14, 15, and 16. With the instructor, review each incorrect response to ensure complete understanding before taking the Stage I Exam in Ground Lesson 6.

STUDY ASSIGNMENT

Private Pilot Textbook/e-Book
Review Chapters 1 – 5 in preparation for the Stage I Exam.

Private Pilot Online — Jeppesen Learning Center
Review Modules 1 – 5 (GL 1 – 16) in preparation for the Stage I Exam.

GROUND LESSON 6 — STAGE I EXAM

REFERENCES

Private Pilot Textbook/e-Book
Chapters 1 – 5

Private Pilot Online — Jeppesen Learning Center
Modules 1 – 5 (GL 1 – 16)

OBJECTIVE
Demonstrate knowledge of the subjects covered in Ground Lessons 1 – 5.

CONTENT
If using Private Pilot Online in the Jeppesen Learning Center, you will find the Stage I Exam in Module 6.

STAGE I EXAM
❑ Airplane Systems
❑ Aerodynamic Principles
❑ The Flight Environment
❑ Communication and Flight Information

COMPLETION STANDARDS
To complete the lesson and stage, pass the Stage I Exam with a minimum score of 80 percent. With the instructor, review each incorrect response to ensure complete understanding before starting Stage II.

STUDY ASSIGNMENT

Private Pilot Textbook/e-Book
Chapter 6 — Meteorology for Pilots (Sections A, B, C)

Private Pilot Online — Jeppesen Learning Center
Module 7 — Meteorology for Pilots (GL 17, 18, 19)

STAGE I ■ **Ground Training Syllabus**

Stage II

STAGE OBJECTIVES

During this stage, the student explores weather theory, typical weather patterns, and aviation weather hazards. In addition to meteorological theory, the student learns how to obtain and interpret various weather reports, forecasts, and graphic weather products. Finally, the student becomes thoroughly familiar with the FARs as they apply to private pilot operations.

STAGE COMPLETION STANDARDS

This stage is complete when the student passes the Stage II Exam with a minimum score of 80%, and the instructor has reviewed with the student each incorrect response to ensure complete understanding before starting Stage III.

GROUND LESSON 7

REFERENCES

Private Pilot Textbook/e-Book
Chapter 6 — Meteorology for Pilots (Sections A, B, C)

Private Pilot Online — Jeppesen Learning Center
Module 7 — Meteorology for Pilots (GL 17, 18, 19)

OBJECTIVES

Part 141/61 Aeronautical Knowledge
- Recognition of critical weather situations from the ground and in flight and wind shear avoidance:
  ◊ Describe the causes of various weather conditions, frontal systems, weather patterns, and hazardous weather phenomena.
  ◊ Explain how to recognize and avoid weather hazards, including thunderstorms, wind shear, turbulence, and restrictions to visibility.
- Safe and efficient operation of aircraft, including recognition and avoidance of wake turbulence:
  ◊ Recognize how wake is generated.
  ◊ Identify techniques to avoid wake turbulence.

CONTENT

SECTION A — BASIC WEATHER THEORY
GL 17 ONLINE — BASIC WEATHER THEORY
❏ The Atmosphere
❏ Atmospheric Circulation
❏ Atmospheric Pressure

❑ Coriolis Force
❑ Global Wind Patterns
❑ Local Wind Patterns

SECTION B — WEATHER PATTERNS
GL 18 ONLINE — WEATHER PATTERNS
❑ Atmospheric Stability
❑ Temperature Inversions
❑ Moisture
❑ Humidity
❑ Dewpoint
❑ Clouds and Fog
❑ Precipitation
❑ Air Masses
❑ Fronts

SECTION C — WEATHER HAZARDS
GL 19 ONLINE — WEATHER HAZARDS
❑ Thunderstorms
❑ Turbulence
❑ Wake Turbulence
❑ Wind Shear
❑ Icing
❑ Restrictions to Visibility
❑ Volcanic Ash

COMPLETION STANDARDS
• Demonstrate understanding of basic weather theory, weather patterns, and weather hazards during oral quizzing by the instructor.
• Complete with a minimum score of 80 percent: questions for Chapter 6A, 6B, and 6C; or online exams for GL 17, 18, and 19. With the instructor, review each incorrect response to ensure complete understanding before starting Ground Lesson 8.

STUDY ASSIGNMENT
FAR/AIM Manual/e-Book
Private Pilot FARs

Private Pilot Online — Jeppesen Learning Center
Module 9 — Federal Aviation Regulations (FARs) (GL 23, 24)

STAGE II ■ Ground Training Syllabus

GROUND LESSON 8

REFERENCES

FAR/AIM Manual/e-Book
Private Pilot FARs

Private Pilot Online — Jeppesen Learning Center
Module 9 — Federal Aviation Regulations (FARs) (GL 23, 24)

OBJECTIVES
Part 141/61 Aeronautical Knowledge
- Applicable Federal Aviation Regulations (FARs) for private pilot privileges, limitations, and flight operations:
  ◊ Explain the regulations that apply to solo operations and the requirements for private pilot certification and currency in FAR Part 61.
  ◊ Explain the general operating and flight rules that apply to VFR operations in FAR Part 91.
- Accident reporting requirements of the National Transportation Safety Board (NTSB):
  ◊ Define the terms used in NTSB 830.
  ◊ List the incidents that require NTSB notification and the information that must be given in notification.

CONTENT
- ❏ FAR Part 1
- ❏ FAR Part 61
- ❏ FAR Part 91
- ❏ NTSB 830

COMPLETION STANDARDS
- Demonstrate understanding of the relevant regulations in 14 CFR (FAR) Part 1, 61, 91, and 49 CFR (NTSB) 830 during oral quizzing by the instructor.
- If using the Private Pilot online course, complete the online exams for GL 23 and 24 with a minimum score of 80 percent. With the instructor, review each incorrect response to ensure complete understanding before starting Ground Lesson 9.

STUDY ASSIGNMENT

Private Pilot Textbook/e-Book
Chapter 7 — Interpreting Weather Data (Sections A, B, C, D)

Private Pilot Online — Jeppesen Learning Center
Module 8 — Interpreting Weather Data (GL 20, 21, 22)

GROUND LESSON 9

REFERENCES

Private Pilot Textbook/e-Book
Chapter 7 — Interpreting Weather Data (Sections A, B, C, D)

Private Pilot Online — Jeppesen Learning Center
Module 8 — Interpreting Weather Data (GL 20, 21, 22)

OBJECTIVES

Part 141/61 Aeronautical Knowledge

- Recognition of critical weather situations from the ground and in flight and the procurement and use of aeronautical weather reports and forecasts:
  ◊ Explain how to obtain weather reports, forecasts, and graphic products.
  ◊ Interpret weather reports and forecasts, including recognizing critical weather conditions.
- Preflight action that includes how to obtain weather reports and forecasts:
  ◊ Identify preflight and inflight weather sources, including Flight Service.
  ◊ Recognize how to acquire weather data for a specific flight, including obtaining an adequate briefing.

CONTENT

SECTION A — THE FORECASTING PROCESS
GL 20 ONLINE — PRINTED REPORTS AND FORECASTS
❑ Forecasting Methods
❑ Compiling and Processing Weather Data
❑ Forecasting Accuracy and Limitations

SECTION B — PRINTED REPORTS AND FORECASTS
GL 20 — PRINTED WEATHER REPORTS AND FORECASTS
❑ Aviation Routine Weather Report (METAR)
❑ Radar Weather Reports
❑ Pilot Weather Reports (PIREPs)
❑ Terminal Aerodrome Forecast (TAF)
❑ Winds and Temperatures Aloft Forecast
❑ Severe Weather Reports and Forecasts
❑ AIRMET/SIGMET/Convective SIGMET

SECTION C — GRAPHIC WEATHER PRODUCTS
GL 21 — GRAPHIC WEATHER REPORTS AND FORECASTS
❑ Surface Analysis Chart
❑ Weather Depiction Chart
❑ Radar Charts and Images
❑ Satellite Weather Pictures
❑ Significant Weather (SIGWX) Prognostic Charts

STAGE II ■ **Ground Training Syllabus**

❏ Convective Outlook Chart
❏ National Convective Weather Forecast
❏ Forecast Winds and Temperatures Aloft
❏ Current and Forecast Icing Products
❏ Ceiling and Visibility Analysis
❏ Volcanic Ash Forecast and Dispersion Chart

SECTION D — SOURCES OF
GL 22 — SOURCES OF WEATHER INFORMATION

❏ Preflight Weather Sources
❏ Flight Service
❏ In-Flight Weather Sources
❏ Automated Weather Reporting Systems
❏ Data Link Weather
❏ Airborne Weather Radar

COMPLETION STANDARDS

• Demonstrate understanding of the forecasting process, printed reports and forecasts, graphic weather products and sources of weather information during oral quizzing by the instructor.
• Complete with a minimum score of 80 percent: questions for Chapter 7A, 7B, and 7C, and 7D; or online exams for GL 20, 21, and 22. With the instructor, review each incorrect response to ensure complete understanding before taking the Stage II Exam in Ground Lesson 10.

STUDY ASSIGNMENT

Private Pilot and FAR/AIM Books/e-Books
Review Chapters 6 and 7, and the FARs that apply to private pilots in preparation for the Stage II Exam.

Private Pilot Online — Jeppesen Learning Center
Review Modules 7 – 9 (GL 17 – 24) in preparation for the Stage II Exam.

GROUND LESSON 10
STAGE II EXAM

REFERENCES

Private Pilot Textbook/e-Book
Chapters 6 and 7

FAR/AIM Manual/e-Book
Private Pilot FARs

Private Pilot Online — Jeppesen Learning Center
Modules 7 – 9 (GL 17 – 24)

OBJECTIVE
Demonstrate knowledge of the subjects covered in Ground Lessons 7 – 9.

CONTENT

If using Private Pilot Online in the Jeppesen Learning Center, you will find the Stage II Exam in Module 10.

STAGE II EXAM
❑ Meteorology for Pilots
❑ Federal Aviation Regulations
❑ Interpreting Weather Data

STUDY ASSIGNMENT

Private Pilot Textbook/e-Book
Chapter 8 — Airplane Performance (Sections A, B, C)

Private Pilot Online — Jeppesen Learning Center
Module 11 — Airplane Performance (GL 25, 26, 27)

COMPLETION STANDARDS
This lesson and stage are complete when the student passes the Stage II Exam with a minimum score of 80%, and the instructor has reviewed with the student each incorrect response to ensure complete understanding before starting Stage III.

STAGE II ■ **Ground Training Syllabus**

Stage III

STAGE OBJECTIVES

During this stage, the student learns how to predict performance and control the weight and balance condition of the airplane. In addition, the student explores pilotage, dead reckoning, VOR, and GPS navigation. The student learns how to calculate aircraft weight and balance and performance, as well as plan flights using aeronautical charts, flight computers, and navigation logs. In addition, the student discovers the physiological factors that can affect both the pilot and passengers during flight. Finally, the student learns how to conduct comprehensive preflight planning for cross-country flights, including using SRM tools to manage risk and make effective decision.

STAGE COMPLETION STANDARDS

This stage is complete when the student passes the Stage III Exam with a minimum score of 80%, and the instructor has reviewed with the student each incorrect response to ensure complete understanding before administering the End-of-Course Final Exams.

GROUND LESSON 11

REFERENCES

Private Pilot Textbook/e-Book
Chapter 8 — Airplane Performance (Sections A, B, C)

Private Pilot Online — Jeppesen Learning Center
Module 11 — Airplane Performance (GL 25, 26, 27)

OBJECTIVES

Part 141/61 Aeronautical Knowledge
- Preflight action that includes how to obtain data on takeoff and landing distances and fuel requirements / effects of density altitude on takeoff and climb performance:
  ◊ Use data supplied by the manufacturer to predict airplane performance, including takeoff and landing distances and fuel requirements.
  ◊ Use a flight computer to calculate airplane performance, such as time, speed, distance, and fuel consumption.
- Weight and balance computations:
  ◊ Compute and control the weight and balance condition of a typical training airplane.
  ◊ Recognize the effects of operating at high total weights and with the center of gravity (CG) at positions near the forward and aft limits.

STAGE III ■ Ground Training Syllabus

CONTENT

SECTION A — PREDICTING PERFORMANCE
GL 26 ONLINE — PREDICTING PERFORMANCE
- ❏ Aircraft Performance and Design
- ❏ Chart Presentations
- ❏ Factors Affecting Aircraft Performance
- ❏ Takeoff and Landing Performance
- ❏ Climb Performance
- ❏ Cruise Performance

SECTION B — WEIGHT AND BALANCE
GL 25 ONLINE — WEIGHT AND BALANCE
- ❏ Importance of Weight
- ❏ Importance of Balance
- ❏ Weight and Balance Terms
- ❏ Principles of Weight and Balance
- ❏ Determining Total Weight and Center of Gravity
  - ◊ Computation Method
  - ◊ Table Method
  - ◊ Graph Method
  - ◊ Weight-Shift Formula
- ❏ Effects of Operating at High Total Weights
- ❏ Flight at Various CG Positions

SECTION C — FLIGHT COMPUTERS
GL 27 ONLINE — MECHANICAL FLIGHT COMPUTERS
- ❏ Mechanical Flight Computers
- ❏ Time, Speed, and Distance
- ❏ Fuel Consumption
- ❏ Airspeed and Density Altitude Computations
- ❏ Wind Problems
- ❏ Conversions
- ❏ Electronic Flight Computers

COMPLETION STANDARDS
- Calculate weight and balance and determine airplane performance under a variety of conditions and explain the results during oral quizzing by the instructor.
- Complete with a minimum score of 80 percent: questions for Chapter 8A, 8B, and 8C; or online exams for GL 25, 26, and 27. With the instructor, review each incorrect response to ensure complete understanding before starting Ground Lesson 12.

STUDY ASSIGNMENT

Private Pilot Textbook/e-Book
  Chapter 9 — Navigation (Sections A, B, C)

Private Pilot Online — Jeppesen Learning Center
  Module 12 — Navigation (GL 28, 29, 30, 31)

STAGE III ■ Ground Training Syllabus

GROUND LESSON 12

REFERENCES

Private Pilot Textbook/e-Book
Chapter 9 — Navigation (Sections A, B, C)

Private Pilot Online — Jeppesen Learning Center
Module 12 — Navigation (GL 28, 29, 30, 31)

OBJECTIVES

Part 141/61 Aeronautical Knowledge
- Applicable Federal Aviation Regulations for flight operations:
  ◊ Plan a VFR flight using pilotage, dead reckoning, and navigation aids, considering fuel reserves and the appropriate VFR cruising altitude.
  ◊ Create a nav log and fill out a flight plan form.
- Applicable subjects of the Aeronautical Information Manual and the appropriate FAA advisory circulars:
  ◊ Explain the operation of navigation aids—VOR and GPS.
  ◊ Interpret navigation aids—VOR and GPS—for VFR navigation.
- How to plan for alternatives if the planned flight cannot be completed or delays are encountered.
  ◊ Identify the steps to perform lost procedures.
  ◊ Recognize how to monitor your flight progress and the actions to take if your flight is delayed or cannot be completed as planned.

CONTENT

SECTION A — PILOTAGE AND DEAD RECKONING
GL 28 ONLINE — PILOTAGE AND DEAD RECKONING
❑ Pilotage
❑ Dead Reckoning
❑ VFR Cruising Altitudes
❑ Flight Planning
❑ VFR Flight Plan
❑ Lost Procedures

SECTION B — VOR NAVIGATION
GL 29 ONLINE — VOR NAVIGATION
GL 31 ONLINE — ADF NAVIGATION
❑ Ground Equipment
❑ Airborne Equipment
❑ Navigation Procedures
❑ Checking VOR Accuracy
❑ Horizontal Situation Indicator (HSI)
❑ Distance Measuring Equipment (DME)
❑ ADF Navigation

STAGE III ■ Ground Training Syllabus

ADF navigation content is optional based on the instructor's discretion, flight environment, and aircraft equipment.

SECTION C — SATELLITE NAVIGATION — GPS
GL 30 ONLINE — GPS NAVIGATION
- ❏ GPS Operation
- ❏ WAAS
- ❏ RAIM
- ❏ Navigating with GPS
- ❏ Navigation Database
- ❏ Course Deviation Indicator (CDI)
- ❏ Moving Map
- ❏ Waypoints
- ❏ GPS Flight Planning
- ❏ Navigation Data
- ❏ Intercepting and Tracking a Course

COMPLETION STANDARDS
- Complete a nav log and flight plan as assigned by the instructor and demonstrate understanding of pilotage and dead reckoning during oral quizzing by the instructor.
- Demonstrate understanding of VOR navigation, GPS navigation, and ADF navigation (if applicable), during oral quizzing by the instructor.
- Complete with a minimum score of 80 percent: questions for Chapter 9A, 9B, and 9C; or online exams for GL 28, 29, 30 (the online course does not test on ADF navigation). With the instructor, review each incorrect response to ensure complete understanding before starting Ground Lesson 13.

STUDY ASSIGNMENT

Private Pilot Textbook/e-Book
Chapter 10 — Applying Human Factors Principles (Sections A, B)

Private Pilot Online — Jeppesen Learning Center
Module 13 — Applying Human Factors Principles (GL 32, 33)

GROUND LESSON 13

REFERENCES

Private Pilot Textbook/e-Book
Chapter 10 — Applying Human Factors Principles (Sections A, B)

Private Pilot Online — Jeppesen Learning Center
Module 13 — Applying Human Factors Principles (GL 32, 33)

STAGE III ■ **Ground Training Syllabus**

OBJECTIVES

Part 141/61 Aeronautical Knowledge
- Applicable subjects of the Aeronautical Information Manual and the appropriate FAA advisory circulars:
  ◊ Recognize how the body functions in flight, including the limitations of vision, disorientation, and respiration.
  ◊ Identify the causes, symptoms, and treatments for hypoxia and hyperventilation.
- Aeronautical decision making and judgment:
  ◊ Explain how to use the tools and techniques of SRM to perform these tasks: risk management, task management, maintain situational awareness, CFIT awareness, and automation management.
  ◊ Apply the aeronautical decision making process to make effective choices during flight operations.

CONTENT

SECTION A — AVIATION PHYSIOLOGY
❑ Vision in Flight
❑ Night Vision
❑ Visual Illusions
❑ Disorientation
❑ Respiration
❑ Hypoxia
❑ Hyperventilation

SECTION B — SINGLE-PILOT RESOURCE MANAGEMENT (SRM)
❑ Accidents and Incidents
❑ Aeronautical Decision Making (ADM)
❑ Self-Assessment
❑ Hazardous Attitudes
❑ Risk Management
❑ Task Management
❑ Situational Awareness
❑ CFIT Awareness
❑ Automation Management
❑ Applying SRM

COMPLETION STANDARDS

- Demonstrate understanding of aviation physiology and SRM tools and techniques during oral quizzing by the instructor.
- Complete with a minimum score of 80 percent: questions for Chapter 10A and 10B; or online exams for GL 32 and 33. Review with the instructor each incorrect response to ensure complete understanding before starting Ground Lesson 14.

STUDY ASSIGNMENT

Private Pilot Textbook/e-Book
  Chapter 11 — Flying Cross-Country (Sections A, B)

Private Pilot Online — Jeppesen Learning Center
  Module 14 — Flying Cross-Country (GL 34, 35)

GROUND LESSON 14

REFERENCES

Private Pilot Textbook/e-Book
  Chapter 11 — Flying Cross-Country (Sections A, B)

Private Pilot Online — Jeppesen Learning Center
  Module 14 — Flying Cross-Country (GL 34, 35)

OBJECTIVES

Part 141/61 Aeronautical Knowledge
- Preflight actions that include (1) how to obtain information on runway lengths at airports of intended use, data on takeoff and landing distances, weather reports and forecasts, and fuel requirements; and (2) how to plan for alternatives if the planned flight cannot be completed or delays are encountered:
  ◊ Gain proficiency in planning a cross-country flight.
  ◊ Identify the tasks that apply to flying a typical cross-country flight, including locating checkpoints, making in-flight time and fuel calculations, and evaluating weather conditions.
  ◊ Recognize how to make and implement decisions regarding alternative actions during a cross-country flight, such as implementing a diversion.
- Applicable subjects of the Aeronautical Information Manual and the appropriate FAA advisory circulars; applicable Federal Aviation Regulations for private pilot privileges, limitations, and flight operations:
  ◊ Identify the pilot responsibilities that apply to planning and performing a cross-country flight.
  ◊ Apply knowledge of airport operations, airspace, ATC services, and flight information sources to plan and perform a cross-country flight.

CONTENT

SECTION A — THE FLIGHT PLANNING PROCESS
GL 34 ONLINE— THE FLIGHT PLANNING PROCESS
❑ Perform a Flight Overview
❑ Develop the Route
❑ Obtain a Weather Briefing
❑ Complete the Nav Log
❑ File the Flight Plan
❑ Perform Preflight Tasks

SECTION B — THE FLIGHT
GL 35 ONLINE — THE FLIGHT
❑ Predeparture
❑ Climb and Initial Cruise
❑ Enroute
❑ Diversion
❑ Descent
❑ Before Approach and Landing
❑ Postflight

STUDY ASSIGNMENT
Private Pilot Textbook/e-Book
 Review Chapters 8 – 11 in preparation for the Stage III Exam.

Private Pilot Online — Jeppesen Learning Center
 Review Modules 11 – 14 in preparation for the Stage III Exam.

COMPLETION STANDARDS
• Demonstrate understanding of the flight planning process and of flying a cross-country during oral quizzing by the instructor.
• Complete with a minimum score of 80 percent: questions for Chapter 11A and 11B; or online exams for GL 34 and 35. Review with the instructor each incorrect response to ensure complete understanding before taking the Stage III Exam in Ground Lesson 15.

GROUND LESSON 15
STAGE III EXAM

REFERENCES

Private Pilot Textbook/e-Book
 Chapters 8 – 11

Private Pilot Online — Jeppesen Learning Center
 Modules 11 – 14 (GL 25 – 35)

OBJECTIVE
Demonstrate knowledge of the subjects covered in Ground Lessons 11 – 14.

CONTENT
If using Private Pilot Online in the Jeppesen Learning Center, you will find the Stage III Exam in Module 15.

STAGE III EXAM
❑ Airplane Performance

❑ Navigation
❑ Applying Human Factors Principles
❑ Flying Cross-Country

STUDY ASSIGNMENT

Private Pilot Textbook/e-Book

Private Pilot Online — Jeppesen Learning Center

Review the entire textbook or online course, as necessary, in preparation for the End-of-Course Final Exam "A."

COMPLETION STANDARDS

This stage is complete when the student passes the Stage III Exam with a minimum score of 80%, and the instructor has reviewed with the student each incorrect response to ensure complete understanding before administering the End-of-Course Final Exams.

GROUND LESSON 16
END-OF-COURSE FINAL EXAM "A"

REFERENCES

Private Pilot Textbook/e-Book
Chapters 1 – 11

Private Pilot Online — Jeppesen Learning Center
Modules 1 – 14 (GL 1 – 35)

OBJECTIVE

Demonstrate comprehension of the material presented in this course in preparation for the FAA Private Pilot Airman Knowledge Test.

CONTENT
❑ Private Pilot End-of-Course Final Exam "A"

STUDY ASSIGNMENT

Review any deficient subject areas based on the results of End-of-Course Final Exam "A." Review in preparation for End-of-Course Final Exam "B."

COMPLETION STANDARDS

Complete the End-of-Course Final Exam "A" with a minimum score of 80% and review with the instructor each incorrect response to ensure complete understanding before taking the End-of-Course Final Exam "B."

GROUND LESSON 17
END-OF-COURSE FINAL EXAM "B"

REFERENCES

Private Pilot Textbook/e-Book
Chapters 1 – 11

Private Pilot Online — Jeppesen Learning Center
Modules 1 – 14 (GL 1 – 35)

OBJECTIVES
Demonstrate comprehension of the material presented in this course in preparation for the FAA Private Pilot Airman Knowledge Test.

CONTENT
❏ Private Pilot End-of-Course Final Exam "B"

STUDY ASSIGNMENT
Review any deficient subject areas based on the results of End-of-Course Final Exam "B." Review in preparation for the FAA Private Pilot Airman Knowledge Test.

COMPLETION STANDARDS
Complete the End-of-Course Final Exam "B" with a minimum score of 80% and review with the instructor each incorrect response to ensure complete understanding so that the instructor can provide recommendation to take the FAA Private Pilot Airman Knowledge Test.

Private Pilot Flight Training Syllabus

FLIGHT TRAINING COURSE OBJECTIVES

The student will obtain the aeronautical skill and experience necessary to meet the requirements for a private pilot certificate with an airplane category rating and single-engine land class rating.

FLIGHT TRAINING COURSE COMPLETION STANDARDS

The student must demonstrate through flight tests and school records that the necessary aeronautical skill and experience requirements to obtain a private pilot certificate with an airplane category rating and single-engine land class rating have been met.

NOTE: Throughout the flight training course, the student must apply and be evaluated on single-pilot resource management (SRM) skills, including aeronautical decision-making (ADM), and risk management. The student must be able to counteract hazardous attitudes, apply the ADM process to make effective decisions, identify hazards and mitigate risks. In addition, the student must demonstrate the ability to manage tasks and automation, maintain situational awareness, and take actions to prevent controlled flight into terrain (CFIT).

Stage I

STAGE OBJECTIVES

During this stage, the student obtains the foundation for all future aviation training. The student becomes familiar with the training airplane and learns how to use the airplane controls to establish and maintain specific flight attitudes and ground tracks. The student learns how to recognize and recover from stalls, and gains the proficiency to solo the training airplane in the traffic pattern.

STAGE COMPLETION STANDARDS

This stage is complete when the student demonstrates proficiency in basic flight maneuvers, and has successfully soloed in the traffic pattern (unless the Stage I Check precedes the first solo flight lesson, in which case, the first solo flight lesson moves to Stage II). In addition, the student must demonstrate the proficiency required for the introduction of short- and soft-field takeoffs and landings in Stage II.

FLIGHT LESSON 1
DUAL — LOCAL (0.5)

NOTE: As indicated in the Allocation Tables, complete Ground Lessons 1 and 2 prior to this flight.

OBJECTIVES
- Become familiar with the training airplane and its systems.
- Identify the certificates and documents that are required to be in the airplane.
- Perform the preflight assessment, including a self-assessment and preflight inspection.
- Use checklists to perform the preflight inspection, start the engine, and perform the before takeoff check, as well as the after landing, parking, and securing procedures.
- Use the rudder pedals and brakes properly to taxi the airplane.
- Use the flight controls to maintain specific attitudes.

PREFLIGHT DISCUSSION
❑ Fitness for Flight
❑ Medical Certificate Class and Duration
❑ Pilot Logbook and Recordkeeping
❑ Private Pilot Privileges, Limitations, and Currency
❑ Aircraft Logbooks
❑ Airplane Servicing

INTRODUCE

PREFLIGHT PREPARATION
❑ Pilot Qualifications
❑ Airworthiness Requirements
❑ Airplane Servicing
❑ Location of First Aid Kit
❑ Location of Fire Extinguisher

PREFLIGHT PROCEDURES
❑ Self-Assessment
❑ Preflight Inspection
❑ Passenger Briefing
❑ Flight Deck Management
❑ Operation of Systems
❑ Use of Checklists
❑ Engine Starting
❑ Before Takeoff Check/Runup

AIRPORT OPERATIONS
❑ Airport Security
❑ Taxiing

TAKEOFFS, LANDINGS, AND GO-AROUNDS
- ❑ Takeoff Briefing
- ❑ Before Landing Briefing
- ❑ Normal Takeoff and Climb
- ❑ Normal Approach and Landing

BASIC MANEUVERS
- ❑ Positive Exchange of Flight Controls
- ❑ Collision Avoidance
- ❑ Use of Trim Control
- ❑ Straight-and-Level Flight
- ❑ Climbs and Descents
- ❑ Turns in Both Directions

POSTFLIGHT PROCEDURES
- ❑ After Landing, Parking, and Securing

COMPLETION STANDARDS
- Display basic knowledge of aircraft systems and the necessity of checking their operation before flight.
- Demonstrate familiarity with the control systems and how to use them to maneuver the airplane on the ground and in flight.

POSTFLIGHT DEBRIEFING
- ❑ Critique maneuvers/procedures and SRM.
- ❑ Update the record folder and logbook.

STUDY ASSIGNMENT

Ground Lesson 3
Aerodynamic Principles

Private Pilot Maneuvers Manual/e-Book
Ground Operations and Basic Maneuvers

Maneuvers Lessons, Private Pilot Online — Jeppesen Learning Center
ML01 — Straight-and-Level Flight
ML02 — Climbs
ML03 — Descents
ML04 — Turns

STAGE I ■ **Flight Training Syllabus**

FLIGHT LESSON 2
DUAL — LOCAL (1.0)

REFERENCES

Private Pilot Maneuvers Manual/e-Book
Ground Operations and Basic Maneuvers

Private Pilot Online — Jeppesen Learning Center
Maneuvers Lessons 1, 2, 3, 4 — Basic Maneuvers

OBJECTIVES
- Use the flight controls to counteract the effects of wind during taxi.
- Adjust pitch and power to maintain various airspeeds.
- Learn how to perform climbing and descending turns to headings.
- Become familiar with the procedures for runway incursion avoidance.
- Gain proficiency in preflight activities, ground operations, and attitude control during basic maneuvers using visual reference (VR).

PREFLIGHT DISCUSSION
- ❏ Human Factors Concepts
- ❏ Single-Pilot Resource Management (SRM)
- ❏ Aeronautical Decision Making (ADM)
- ❏ Runway Incursion Avoidance
- ❏ Airport, Runway, and Taxiway Signs, Markings, and Lighting
- ❏ Airspeed and Configuration Changes

INTRODUCE

AIRPORT OPERATIONS
- ❏ Airport, Runway, and Taxiway Signs, Markings, and Lighting
- ❏ Runway Incursion Avoidance
- ❏ Radio Communications
- ❏ Traffic Patterns/Departure, Arrival, Entry, and Approach Procedures

BASIC MANEUVERS
- ❏ Flight at Various Airspeeds from Cruise to Slow Flight
- ❏ Turns to Headings
- ❏ Climbs and Climbing Turns
- ❏ Descents and Descending Turns in High and Low Drag Configurations

REVIEW

PREFLIGHT PREPARATION
- ❏ Pilot Qualifications
- ❏ Airworthiness Requirements
- ❏ Airplane Servicing

❏ Location of First Aid Kit
❏ Location of Fire Extinguisher

PREFLIGHT PROCEDURES
❏ Self-Assessment
❏ Preflight Inspection
❏ Passenger Briefing
❏ Flight Deck Management
❏ Operation of Systems
❏ Use of Checklists
❏ Engine Starting
❏ Before Takeoff Check/Runup

AIRPORT OPERATIONS
❏ Airport Security
❏ Taxiing

BASIC MANEUVERS/PROCEDURES
❏ Positive Exchange of Flight Controls
❏ Collision Avoidance
❏ Use of Trim Control
❏ Straight-and-Level Flight
❏ Climbs and Descents
❏ Turns in Both Directions

TAKEOFFS, LANDINGS, AND GO-AROUNDS
❏ Takeoff Briefing
❏ Before Landing Briefing
❏ Normal Takeoff and Climb
❏ Normal Approach and Landing

POSTFLIGHT PROCEDURES
❏ After Landing, Parking, and Securing

COMPLETION STANDARDS
- Perform the preflight activities, ground operations, and coordinated airplane attitude control with instructor assistance.
- Perform taxiing and takeoffs with instructor assistance.

POSTFLIGHT DEBRIEFING
❏ Critique maneuvers/procedures and SRM.
❏ Create a plan for skills that need improvement.
❏ Update the record folder and logbook.

STUDY ASSIGNMENT

Ground Lesson 4
The Flight Environment

FLIGHT LESSON 3
DUAL — LOCAL (1.0)

NOTE: A view-limiting device is required for the 0.2 hours of dual instrument time allocated to Flight Lesson 3.

REFERENCES

Private Pilot Maneuvers Manual/e-Book
Ground Operations and Basic Maneuvers

Private Pilot Online — Jeppesen Learning Center
Maneuvers Lessons 1, 2, 3, 4 — Basic Maneuvers

OBJECTIVES
- Become familiar with recognition of and recovery from stalls entered from various flight attitudes and power combinations.
- Control the airplane attitude solely by instrument reference (IR).
- Gain proficiency in controlling airspeed during basic maneuvers and traffic pattern operations.

PREFLIGHT DISCUSSION
❏ Task Management
❏ Situational Awareness
❏ Basic Instrument Maneuvers
❏ Wind Shear and Wake Turbulence Avoidance Procedures

INTRODUCE

PREFLIGHT PREPARATION
❏ Human Factors
❏ Weather Information

SLOW FLIGHT AND STALLS
Stall entries from various flight attitudes and power combinations with recovery initiated at the first indication of a stall, and recovery from a full stall
❏ Maneuvering During Slow Flight
❏ Power-Off Stalls
❏ Power-On Stalls

BASIC INSTRUMENT MANEUVERS
Control and maneuvering solely by reference to instruments
❏ Straight-and-Level Flight (IR)
❏ Constant Airspeed Climbs (IR)
❏ Constant Airspeed Descents (IR)
❏ Turns to Headings (IR)

REVIEW

AIRPORT OPERATIONS
- ❑ Airport, Runway, and Taxiway Signs, Markings, and Lighting
- ❑ Runway Incursion Avoidance
- ❑ Radio Communications
- ❑ Traffic Patterns/Departure, Arrival, Entry, and Approach Procedures

BASIC MANEUVERS
- ❑ Airspeed and Flight at Various Airspeeds from Cruise to Slow Flight
- ❑ Turns to Headings
- ❑ Climbs and Climbing Turns
- ❑ Descents and Descending Turns in High and Low Drag Configurations

TAKEOFFS, LANDINGS, AND GO-AROUNDS
- ❑ Takeoff Briefing
- ❑ Before Landing Briefing
- ❑ Normal Takeoff and Climb
- ❑ Normal Approach and Landing

COMPLETION STANDARDS
- Display increased proficiency in attitude control during basic maneuvers.
- Perform unassisted takeoffs.
- Perform correct communications and traffic pattern procedures with instructor assistance.
- Complete landings with instructor assistance.
- Maintain altitude within ± 250 feet during airspeed transitions and while maneuvering at slow airspeeds.
- Control airplane attitude by instrument reference (IR).

POSTFLIGHT DEBRIEFING
- ❑ Critique maneuvers/procedures and SRM.
- ❑ Create a plan for skills that need improvement.
- ❑ Update the record folder and logbook.

Study Assignment Ground Lesson 5
Communication & Flight Information

Private Pilot Maneuvers Manual/e-Book
Flight Maneuvers, Emergency Operations, and Special Flight Operations: Basic Instrument Maneuvers

Maneuvers Lessons, Private Pilot Online — Jeppesen Learning Center
ML05 — Slow Flight
ML06 — Stalls
ML07 — Steep Turns
ML08 — Attitude Instrument Flying
ML11 — Systems and Equipment Malfunctions
ML12 — Emergency Descent
ML13 — Emergency Approach and Landing

STAGE I ■ **Flight Training Syllabus**

FLIGHT LESSON 4
DUAL — LOCAL (1.0)

NOTE: A view-limiting device is required for the 0.2 hours of dual instrument time allocated to Flight Lesson 4.

NOTE: All preflight duties and procedures will be performed and evaluated prior to each flight. Therefore, they will not appear in the task lists.

REFERENCES

Private Pilot Maneuvers Manual/e-Book
Flight Maneuvers
Emergency Operations
Special Flight Operations: Basic Instrument Maneuvers

Private Pilot Online — Jeppesen Learning Center
Maneuvers Lessons 5, 6, 7, 8 — Flight Maneuvers
Maneuvers Lessons 11, 12, 13 — Emergency Operations

OBJECTIVES
- Recognize and recover correctly from stalls.
- Learn the procedures for managing system and equipment malfunctions.
- Become familiar with flying an approach to a landing area during simulated engine malfunctions.
- Become familiar with the control inputs and visual references required to perform steep turns.
- Learn about the causes and recovery procedures for secondary, accelerated, cross-control, and elevator trim stalls by observing instructor demonstrations.
- Gain additional proficiency in controlling the airplane by instrument reference (IR).

PREFLIGHT DISCUSSION
❏ Risk Management
❏ Systems and Equipment Malfunctions
❏ Emergency Field Selection
❏ Emergency Equipment and Survival Gear

INTRODUCE

EMERGENCY OPERATIONS
❏ Systems and Equipment Malfunctions
❏ Emergency Descent
❏ Emergency Approach and Landing (Simulated)
❏ Emergency Equipment and Survival Gear

PERFORMANCE MANEUVERS
❏ Steep Turns

BASIC INSTRUMENT MANEUVERS
Control and maneuvering solely by reference to instruments
- ❏ Climbing and Descending Turns (IR)

SLOW FLIGHT AND STALLS
- ❏ Demonstrated Stalls (Secondary, Accelerated, Cross-Control, and Elevator Trim)
- ❏ Spin Awareness

NOTE: The demonstrated stalls are not a proficiency requirement for private pilot certification. The purpose of the demonstrations is to help the student learn how to recognize, prevent, and if necessary, recover before the stall develops into a spin. These stalls should not be practiced without a qualified flight instructor. In addition, certain types of stalls might be prohibited in some airplanes.

REVIEW

PREFLIGHT PREPARATION
- ❏ Human Factors
- ❏ Weather Information

SLOW FLIGHT AND STALLS
Stall entries from various flight attitudes and power combinations with recovery initiated at the first indication of a stall, and recovery from a full stall
- ❏ Maneuvering During Slow Flight
- ❏ Power-Off Stalls
- ❏ Power-On Stalls

BASIC INSTRUMENT MANEUVERS
Control and maneuvering solely by reference to instruments
- ❏ Straight-and-Level Flight (IR)
- ❏ Constant Airspeed Climbs (IR)
- ❏ Constant Airspeed Descents (IR)
- ❏ Turns to Headings (IR)

TAKEOFFS, LANDINGS, AND GO-AROUNDS
- ❏ Normal Takeoffs and Landings

COMPLETION STANDARDS
- Maintain coordinated airplane attitude control during basic maneuvers using both outside visual reference and solely by reference to instruments.
- Perform takeoffs without instructor assistance.
- Demonstrate correct communications and traffic pattern procedures.
- Complete landings with instructor assistance.
- Perform the correct procedures to establish and recover from slow flight and stalls, perform steep turns, and manage emergency situations.
- Explain the causes and recovery procedures for secondary, accelerated, cross-control, and elevator trim stalls, as well as spins.

STAGE I ■ **Flight Training Syllabus**

POSTFLIGHT DEBRIEFING
❑ Critique maneuvers/procedures and SRM.
❑ Create a plan for skills that need improvement.
❑ Update the record folder and logbook.

STUDY ASSIGNMENT

Ground Lesson 6
Stage I Exam

Private Pilot Maneuvers Manual/e-Book
Ground Reference Maneuvers

Maneuvers Lessons, Private Pilot Online — Jeppesen Learning Center
ML09 — Ground Reference Maneuvers

FLIGHT LESSON 5
DUAL — LOCAL (1.0)

NOTE: A view-limiting device is required for the 0.2 hours of dual instrument time allocated to Flight Lesson 5.

REFERENCES

Private Pilot Maneuvers Manual/e-Book
Ground Reference Maneuvers

Private Pilot Online — Jeppesen Learning Center
Maneuvers Lesson 9 — Ground Reference Maneuvers

OBJECTIVES
• Learn how to correct for wind drift and changing groundspeed to maintain a specific ground track by performing ground reference maneuvers.
• Increase proficiency in selecting and maneuvering to a landing site during an emergency approach and landing.
• Gain proficiency in performing slow flight, stalls, and steep turns.

PREFLIGHT DISCUSSION
❑ Situational Awareness
❑ Realistic Distractions
❑ Determining Wind Direction
❑ CFIT Awareness
❑ Wire Strike Avoidance

INTRODUCE

GROUND REFERENCE MANEUVERS
❑ Rectangular Courses
❑ S-Turns

STAGE I ■ Flight Training Syllabus

❏ Turns Around a Point

REVIEW

EMERGENCY OPERATIONS
❏ Systems and Equipment Malfunctions
❏ Emergency Descent
❏ Emergency Approach and Landing (Simulated)
❏ Emergency Equipment and Survival Gear

PERFORMANCE MANEUVERS
❏ Steep Turns

BASIC INSTRUMENT MANEUVERS
Control and maneuvering solely by reference to instruments
❏ Climbing and Descending Turns (IR)

SLOW FLIGHT AND STALLS
Stall entries from various flight attitudes and power combinations with recovery initiated at the first indication of a stall, and recovery from a full stall
❏ Maneuvering During Slow Flight
❏ Power-Off Stalls
❏ Power-On Stalls
❏ Spin Awareness

TAKEOFFS, LANDINGS, AND GO-AROUNDS
❏ Normal Takeoffs and Landings

COMPLETION STANDARDS
• Demonstrate correct communication and traffic pattern procedures.
• Complete landings with minimal instructor assistance.
• Maintain altitude ± 200 feet, headings ± 15°, and airspeed ± 15 knots during basic flight maneuvers (VR and IR).
• Demonstrate understanding of the proper flight techniques and the appropriate wind correction techniques for flying rectangular courses, S-turns, and turns around a point.
• Demonstrate the ability to recognize and recover from stalls.
• Take appropriate actions to manage emergency situations and perform simulated emergency landing procedures.

POSTFLIGHT DEBRIEFING
❏ Critique maneuvers/procedures and SRM.
❏ Create a plan for skills that need improvement.
❏ Update the record folder and logbook.

STUDY ASSIGNMENT

Ground Lesson 7
Meteorology for Pilots

Private Pilot Maneuvers Manual/e-Book
Airport Operations

Maneuvers Lessons, Private Pilot Online — Jeppesen Learning Center
ML10 — Traffic Patterns
ML14 — Normal Takeoff and Climb
ML15 — Normal Approach and Landing
ML16 — Crosswind Takeoff and Landing

STAGE I ■ Flight Training Syllabus

FLIGHT LESSON 6
DUAL — LOCAL (1.0)

REFERENCES

> **Private Pilot Maneuvers Manual/e-Book**
> Airport Operations

> **Private Pilot Online — Jeppesen Learning Center**
> Maneuvers Lessons 10, 14, 15, 16 — Airport Operations

OBJECTIVES
- Learn how to perform forward slips and crosswind takeoffs and landings in varying wind conditions.
- Recognize the need for and the steps to take to perform rejected takeoffs and go-arounds/rejected landings.
- Learn about land and hold short operations (LAHSO) and review procedures for runway incursion avoidance.
- Become familiar with the procedures to avoid wake turbulence wind shear.
- Gain proficiency in ground reference maneuvers.

PREFLIGHT DISCUSSION
❑ Workload Management
❑ Lost Communication Procedures
❑ Runway Incursion Avoidance
❑ Wake Turbulence Avoidance
❑ Wind Shear Avoidance

INTRODUCE

AIRPORT OPERATIONS
❑ Lost Communication Procedures/ATC Light Signals
❑ Wake Turbulence Avoidance
❑ Wind Shear Avoidance

TAKEOFFS, LANDINGS, AND GO-AROUNDS
❑ Rejected Takeoff
❑ Go-Around/Rejected Landing

❑ Forward Slips to Landing
❑ Crosswind Takeoff and Climb
❑ Crosswind Approach and Landing

REVIEW

GROUND REFERENCE MANEUVERS
❑ Rectangular Courses
❑ S-Turns
❑ Turns Around a Point

COMPLETION STANDARDS
- Fly a specific ground track while maintaining altitude ± 200 feet.
- Use the proper control application to perform a forward slip to a landing.
- Perform rejected takeoffs, crosswind takeoff/landing procedures, and go-arounds with instructor assistance.
- Explain and follow the procedures for runway incursion avoidance, land and hold short operations (LAHSO), wake turbulence avoidance, and wind shear avoidance.

POSTFLIGHT DEBRIEFING
❑ Critique maneuvers/procedures and SRM.
❑ Create a plan for skills that need improvement.
❑ Update the record folder and logbook.

STUDY ASSIGNMENT

Ground Lesson 8
Federal Aviation Regulations

Private Pilot Maneuvers Manual/e-Book
Review Maneuvers 1 – 16 and 32

Maneuvers Lessons, Private Pilot Online — Jeppesen Learning Center
Review Maneuvers 1 – 16

FLIGHT LESSON 7
DUAL — LOCAL (1.0)

NOTE: A view-limiting device is required for the 0.2 hours of dual instrument time allocated to Flight Lesson 7

REFERENCES

Private Pilot Maneuvers Manual/e-Book
Review Maneuvers 1 – 16 and 32

Private Pilot Online — Jeppesen Learning Center
Maneuvers 1 – 16

OBJECTIVES

Prepare for the first solo flight by demonstrating proficiency in performing:

- Basic flight maneuvers, takeoffs, landings, rejected takeoffs, go-arounds, and emergency procedures.
- Slow flight and stalls.
- Basic maneuvers solely by reference to instruments.
- Ground reference maneuvers.

PREFLIGHT DISCUSSION

❏ Sections of FAR Parts 61 and 91—that apply to student and private pilots
❏ Airspace Rules and Procedures—for the airport where solo flight will be performed
❏ Flight Characteristics and Operational Limitations—for the make and model of aircraft to be flown in solo flight

REVIEW

AIRPORT OPERATIONS

❏ Airport Security
❏ Taxiing
❏ Airport, Runway, and Taxiway Signs, Markings, and Lighting
❏ Runway Incursion Avoidance
❏ Radio Communications
❏ Traffic Patterns/Departure, Arrival, Entry, and Approach Procedures
❏ Lost Communication Procedures/ATC Light Signals
❏ Wake Turbulence Avoidance
❏ Wind Shear Avoidance

EMERGENCY OPERATIONS

❏ Systems and Equipment Malfunctions
❏ Emergency Descent
❏ Emergency Approach and Landing (Simulated)
❏ Emergency Equipment and Survival Gear

PERFORMANCE MANEUVERS

❏ Steep Turns

BASIC INSTRUMENT MANEUVERS

Control and maneuvering solely by reference to instruments
❏ Straight-and-Level Flight (IR)
❏ Constant Airspeed Climbs (IR)
❏ Constant Airspeed Descents (IR)
❏ Turns to Headings (IR)
❏ Climbing and Descending Turns (IR)

SLOW FLIGHT AND STALLS

Stall entries from various flight attitudes and power combinations with recovery initiated at the first indication of a stall, and recovery from a full stall
❏ Maneuvering During Slow Flight

- ❑ Power-Off Stalls
- ❑ Power-On Stalls
- ❑ Spin Awareness

GROUND REFERENCE MANEUVERS
- ❑ Rectangular Courses
- ❑ S-Turns
- ❑ Turns Around a Point

TAKEOFFS, LANDINGS, AND GO-AROUNDS
- ❑ Rejected Takeoff
- ❑ Go-Around/Rejected Landing
- ❑ Forward Slips to Landing
- ❑ Normal and Crosswind Takeoffs and Landings

COMPLETION STANDARDS
- Display increased proficiency and skill in instrument scan and interpretation during practice of basic instrument maneuvers.
- Perform takeoffs, landings, and go-arounds at a safe airspeed without instructor assistance.
- Perform emergency procedures with minimal instructor assistance.
- Maintain altitude and properly adjust bank angle to correct for wind effects when performing ground reference maneuvers.

POSTFLIGHT DEBRIEFING
- ❑ Critique maneuvers/procedures and SRM.
- ❑ Create a plan for skills that need improvement.
- ❑ Update the record folder and logbook.

STUDY ASSIGNMENT

Ground Lesson 9
 Interpreting Weather Data

Prepare for the Presolo Exam and Briefing. The student will be provided with the exam questions in advance.

FLIGHT LESSON 8
DUAL — LOCAL (1.0)

NOTE: A view-limiting device is required for the 0.2 hours of dual instrument time allocated to Flight Lesson 8.

NOTE: Presolo briefing questions are included in Appendix A.

OBJECTIVES
- Grade the Presolo Exam and conduct the Presolo Briefing.
- Demonstrate proficiency in airport operations, takeoffs, and landings in preparation for the first solo flight.

- Increase proficiency and confidence in performing review maneuvers, procedures, and emergency operations.

PREFLIGHT DISCUSSION
❏ Presolo Exam Critique
❏ Presolo Flight Training Requirements

REVIEW

AIRPORT OPERATIONS
❏ Airport Security
❏ Taxiing
❏ Airport, Runway, and Taxiway Signs, Markings, and Lighting
❏ Runway Incursion Avoidance
❏ Radio Communications
❏ Traffic Patterns/Departure, Arrival, Entry, and Approach Procedures
❏ Lost Communication Procedures/ATC Light Signals
❏ Wake Turbulence Avoidance
❏ Wind Shear Avoidance

EMERGENCY OPERATIONS
❏ Systems and Equipment Malfunctions
❏ Emergency Approach and Landing (Simulated)

TAKEOFFS, LANDINGS, AND GO-AROUNDS
❏ Rejected Takeoff
❏ Go-Around/Rejected Landing
❏ Forward Slips to Landing
❏ Normal and Crosswind Takeoffs and Landings

COMPLETION STANDARDS
- Successfully pass the Presolo Exam with a minimum score of 80%, and with the instructor, review each incorrect response to ensure complete understanding.
- Demonstrate ability and readiness for solo flight in the traffic pattern.
- Consistently perform takeoffs and climbs, approaches and landings, rejected takeoffs, and go-arounds safely and without instructor assistance.
- Control and maneuver the airplane solely by reference to instruments.
- Explain local airport and airspace rules.
- Effectively manage systems and equipment malfunctions and perform the correct emergency procedures.
- Maintain altitude ± 150 feet, headings ± 15°, and airspeed ± 10 knots.

POSTFLIGHT DEBRIEFING
❏ Critique maneuvers/procedures and SRM.
❏ Create a plan for skills that need improvement.
❏ Update the record folder and logbook.

STUDY ASSIGNMENT

Review any deficient subject areas based on the results of the Presolo Exam. Review the *Private Pilot Maneuvers* manual or online lessons as required, or as assigned by the instructor.

FLIGHT LESSON 9
DUAL — LOCAL (0.5)
SOLO — LOCAL (0.5)

NOTE: This flight becomes the first flight lesson in Stage II after the Stage I Check if that option is selected by marking the applicable check box in the Preface. If that is the case, proceed directly to Flight Lesson 10, the Stage I Check.

NOTE: This flight occurs after the Stage I Check and Flight Lessons 11, 14, and 15 in Stage II if that option is selected by marking the check box in the Preface. If that is the case, proceed directly to Flight Lesson 10, the Stage I Check.

NOTE: Student pilots conducting solo flight operations are not authorized to participate in LAHSO.

OBJECTIVES
- During the dual portion of the lesson, the instructor reviews takeoff and landing procedures to ensure the student's readiness for solo flight.
- During the second portion of the lesson, the student performs the first supervised solo flight in the local traffic pattern.

PREFLIGHT DISCUSSION
❏ Student Questions
❏ Solo Operations in the Traffic Pattern
❏ Single-Pilot Resource Management (SRM)

REVIEW

DUAL
❏ Engine Starting
❏ Radio Communications
❏ Taxiing
❏ Before Takeoff Check/Runup
❏ Normal Takeoff and Climb
❏ Traffic Patterns
❏ Rejected Takeoff
❏ Go-Around/Rejected Landing
❏ Normal Approach and Landing

STAGE I ■ **Flight Training Syllabus**

INTRODUCE

SUPERVISED SOLO
- ❏ Radio Communications
- ❏ Taxiing
- ❏ Before Takeoff Check/Runup
- ❏ Normal Takeoff and Climb (3)
- ❏ Traffic Patterns (3)
- ❏ Normal Approach and Landing (3)
- ❏ After Landing, Parking, and Securing

COMPLETION STANDARDS
- Demonstrate the ability to solo the training airplane safely in the traffic pattern. At no time will the safety of the flight be in question.
- Complete solo flight in the local traffic pattern as directed by the instructor.

POSTFLIGHT DEBRIEFING
- ❏ Critique maneuvers/procedures and SRM.
- ❏ Create a plan for skills that need improvement.
- ❏ Update the record folder and logbook.

STUDY ASSIGNMENT

Ground Lesson 10

Stage II Exam Review, as required, in preparation for the Stage I Check in Flight Lesson 10.

NOTE: If this is the first flight in Stage II, complete the study assignment for performance takeoffs and landings in Flight Lesson 11.

FLIGHT LESSON 10
DUAL — LOCAL (1.0)
STAGE I CHECK

OBJECTIVES
Demonstrate to the chief instructor, the assistant chief instructor, or the designated check instructor:
- Proficiency in the maneuvers, procedures, and knowledge areas required to depart the traffic pattern area on future solo flights.
- Competence in SRM, risk management, and ADM skills applicable to operating solo in the local area.

PREFLIGHT DISCUSSION
Conduct of the Stage I Check, including:
- ❏ Maneuvers
- ❏ Procedures

❑ Acceptable Performance Criteria
❑ Applicable Rules

EVALUATE

PREFLIGHT PREPARATION
❑ Pilot Qualifications
❑ Airworthiness Requirements
❑ Human Factors
❑ Weather Information

PREFLIGHT PROCEDURES
❑ Self-Assessment
❑ Preflight Inspection
❑ Flight Deck Management
❑ Operation of Systems
❑ Use of Checklists
❑ Engine Starting
❑ Before Takeoff Check/Runup

AIRPORT OPERATIONS
❑ Airport Security
❑ Taxiing
❑ Airport, Runway, and Taxiway Signs, Markings, and Lighting
❑ Runway Incursion Avoidance
❑ Radio Communications
❑ Traffic Patterns/Departure, Arrival, Entry, and Approach Procedures
❑ Lost Communication Procedures/ATC Light Signals
❑ Wake Turbulence Avoidance
❑ Wind Shear Avoidance

EMERGENCY OPERATIONS
❑ Systems and Equipment Malfunctions
❑ Emergency Descent
❑ Emergency Approach and Landing (Simulated)
❑ Emergency Equipment and Survival Gear

SLOW FLIGHT AND STALLS
Stall entries from various flight attitudes and power combinations with recovery initiated at the first indication of a stall, and recovery from a full stall
❑ Maneuvering During Slow Flight
❑ Power-Off Stalls
❑ Power-On Stalls
❑ Spin Awareness

GROUND REFERENCE MANEUVERS
❑ Rectangular Courses
❑ S-Turns
❑ Turns Around a Point

STAGE I ■ **Flight Training Syllabus**

TAKEOFFS, LANDINGS, AND GO-AROUNDS
❑ Rejected Takeoff
❑ Go-Around/Rejected Landing
❑ Forward Slips to Landing
❑ Normal and Crosswind Takeoffs and Landings

POSTFLIGHT PROCEDURES
❑ After Landing, Parking, and Securing

COMPLETION STANDARDS

This lesson and Stage I are complete when the student can competently perform preflight duties and all other procedures and maneuvers necessary for the safe conduct of a solo flight in the local training area. The student will maintain altitude ± 150 feet, headings ± 15°, and airspeed ± 10 knots.

POSTFLIGHT DEBRIEFING

❑ Evaluate maneuvers/procedures and SRM.
❑ Plan further instruction for skills not meeting Stage I completion standards.
❑ Update the record folder and logbook.

STUDY ASSIGNMENT

Ground Lesson 11
Airplane Performance

Private Pilot Maneuvers Manual/e-Book
Performance Takeoffs and Landings

Maneuvers Lessons, Private Pilot Online — Jeppesen Learning Center
Private ML17 — Short- and Soft-Field Takeoffs and Landings

Stage II

STAGE OBJECTIVES

During Stage II, the student expands the skills learned in the previous stage. The student is introduced to short-field and soft-field takeoff and landing procedures, as well as night operations, which are important steps in preparation for cross-country training. Additionally, the student will increase proficiency in performing maneuvers and procedures solely by reference to instruments. In the cross-country phase, the student learns to effectively plan and conduct cross-country flights in the National Airspace System using pilotage, dead reckoning, and VOR, GPS, and ADF navigation systems (based on aircraft equipment).

STAGE COMPLETION STANDARDS

At the completion of Stage II, the student has successfully completed the first solo (if the first solo flight lesson occurs in this stage). In addition, the student is able to accurately plan and conduct cross-country flights and can safely and consistently perform short-field and soft-field takeoffs and landings. The student can also plan and implement night flights. The proficiency level must be such that the successful and safe outcome of each task is never in doubt.

FLIGHT LESSON 11
DUAL — LOCAL (1.0)

NOTE: At the instructor's discretion, this lesson may be conducted at a nearby airport in the local area.

REFERENCES

Private Pilot Maneuvers Manual/e-Book
Performance Takeoffs and Landings

Private Pilot Online — Jeppesen Learning Center
Maneuvers Lesson 17 — Performance Takeoffs and Landings

OBJECTIVES
- Learn the procedures for short- and soft-field takeoffs, climbs, approaches, and landings in the training airplane.
- Gain proficiency in ground reference maneuvers, slow flight, and stall recognition and recovery.
- Ensure proficiency for performing the second supervised solo in the traffic pattern.

PREFLIGHT DISCUSSION
❑ Weight and Balance Computations
❑ Performance and Limitations
❑ Effects of High Density Altitude
❑ Land and Hold Short Operations (LAHSO)

INTRODUCE

TAKEOFFS, LANDINGS, AND GO-AROUNDS
❑ Short-Field Takeoff and Maximum-Performance Climb
❑ Soft-Field Takeoff and Climb
❑ Short-Field Approach and Landing
❑ Soft-Field Approach and Landing
❑ Climbs at Best Angle and Best Rate

AIRPORT OPERATIONS
❑ Land and Hold Short Operations (LAHSO)

REVIEW

AIRPORT OPERATIONS
❑ Runway Incursion Avoidance
❑ Radio Communications
❑ Traffic Patterns/Departure, Arrival, Entry, and Approach Procedures
❑ Wake Turbulence Avoidance
❑ Wind Shear Avoidance

COMPLETION STANDARDS
• Explain the runway conditions that necessitate the use of soft-field and short-field takeoff and landing techniques.
• Perform short- and soft-field takeoffs and landings with instructor assistance.

POSTFLIGHT DEBRIEFING
❑ Critique maneuvers/procedures and SRM.
❑ Create a plan for skills that need improvement.
❑ Update the record folder and logbook.

STUDY ASSIGNMENT

Ground Lesson 12
 Navigation

Review, as required, in preparation for Flight Lesson 12, which is the second supervised solo in the traffic pattern.

FLIGHT LESSON 12
SOLO — LOCAL (1.0)

NOTE: At the instructor's discretion, a portion of this lesson may be dual.

NOTE: Student pilots conducting solo flight operations are not authorized to participate in LAHSO.

OBJECTIVES
- Fly the second supervised solo in the local traffic pattern.
- Gain confidence and proficiency in conducting airport operations, including takeoffs, traffic patterns, approach and landing procedures, collision avoidance, and radio communications.

PREFLIGHT DISCUSSION
❑ Student Questions
❑ Solo Operations in the Traffic Pattern
❑ Single-Pilot Resource Management (SRM)

REVIEW

SUPERVISED SOLO
❑ Radio Communications
❑ Taxiing
❑ Before Takeoff Check/Runup
❑ Normal Takeoff and Climb
❑ Traffic Patterns
❑ Normal Approach and Landing
❑ After Landing, Parking, and Securing

COMPLETION STANDARDS
- Rotate and lift off at the recommended airspeed and accelerate to V_Y within +10/-5 knots.
- Establish the recommended approach and landing configuration and airspeed, and adjust pitch attitude and power as required to maintain a stabilized approach with approach speed within +10/-5 knots.
- Make smooth, timely, and correct control inputs during round out and touchdown.

POSTFLIGHT DEBRIEFING
❑ Critique maneuvers/procedures and SRM.
❑ Create a plan for skills that need improvement.
❑ Update the record folder and logbook.

STUDY ASSIGNMENT
Ground Lesson 13
Human Factor Principles

Review, as required, in preparation for the first solo flight in the local flying area.

FLIGHT LESSON 13
SOLO — LOCAL (1.0)

OBJECTIVES
- Increase proficiency in maintaining specific ground tracks by practicing ground reference maneuvers.
- Practice other maneuvers as directed by the flight instructor.
- Improve skills in traffic pattern entry, exit, approach, and landing procedures, including use of a stabilized approach.

REVIEW

AIRPORT OPERATIONS
❑ Radio Communications

SLOW FLIGHT AND STALLS
❑ Maneuvering During Slow Flight
❑ Power-Off Stalls
❑ Power-On Stalls

GROUND REFERENCE MANEUVERS
❑ Rectangular Courses
❑ S-Turns
❑ Turns Around a Point

TAKEOFFS, LANDINGS, AND GO-AROUNDS
❑ Normal and Crosswind Takeoffs and Landings
❑ Short- and Soft-Field Takeoffs and Landings

COMPLETION STANDARDS
- Safely conduct the assigned solo flight.
- Gain proficiency in each of the assigned maneuvers and procedures.

POSTFLIGHT DEBRIEFING
❑ Critique maneuvers and procedures and SRM.
❑ Create a plan for skills that need improvement.
❑ Update the record folder and logbook.

STUDY ASSIGNMENT

Ground Lesson 14
Flying Cross-Country

Private Pilot Maneuvers Manual/e-Book
Review Special Flight Operations: Basic Instrument Maneuvers

Maneuvers Lessons, Private Pilot Online — Jeppesen Learning Center
Review ML08 — Attitude Instrument Flying

FLIGHT LESSON 14
DUAL — LOCAL (1.0)

NOTE: A view-limiting device is required for the 0.5 hours of dual instrument time allocated to Flight Lesson 14.

NOTE: At the instructor's discretion, this lesson may be conducted at a nearby airport in the local area.

REFERENCES

Private Pilot Maneuvers Manual/e-Book
Special Flight Operations: Basic Instrument Maneuvers

Private Pilot Online — Jeppesen Learning Center
Maneuvers Lesson 8 — Attitude Instrument Flying

OBJECTIVES
- Become familiar with navigation using VOR, GPS, and ADF (based on aircraft equipment).
- Become familiar with controlling the airplane solely by reference to instruments while using navigation systems and ATC services.
- Use instrument reference to recognize and recover from unusual attitudes.

PREFLIGHT DISCUSSION
- ❑ Inadvertent VFR Flight into IFR Conditions
- ❑ Spatial Disorientation
- ❑ Task Management
- ❑ Situational Awareness

INTRODUCE

NAVIGATION
- ❑ VOR Navigation
- ❑ GPS Navigation
- ❑ ADF Navigation, based on aircraft equipment
- ❑ Autopilot Use, if equipped

BASIC INSTRUMENT MANEUVERS
Control and maneuvering solely by reference to instruments
- ❑ Recovery from Unusual Flight Attitudes (IR)
- ❑ Using Radio Communications, Navigation Systems/Facilities, and ATC Services Appropriate to Instrument Flight (IR)

REVIEW

AIRPORT OPERATIONS
- ❑ Land and Hold Short Operations (LAHSO)

STAGE II ■ **Flight Training Syllabus**

TAKEOFFS, LANDINGS, AND GO-AROUNDS
- ❑ Short-Field Takeoff and Maximum-Performance Climb
- ❑ Soft-Field Takeoff and Climb
- ❑ Short-Field Approach and Landing
- ❑ Soft-Field Approach and Landing
- ❑ Climbs at Best Angle and Best Rate

COMPLETION STANDARDS
- Perform takeoffs and landings smoothly, maintaining directional control.
- Perform stabilized approaches to landing maintaining the proper airspeed within +10/-5 knots.
- Follow the correct procedures for orientation and tracking using VOR, GPS, and ADF equipment, as applicable to the airplane.
- Perform the correct unusual attitude recovery techniques.

POSTFLIGHT DEBRIEFING
- ❑ Critique maneuvers/procedures and SRM.
- ❑ Create a plan for skills that need improvement.
- ❑ Update the record folder and logbook.

STUDY ASSIGNMENT
Ground Lesson 15
Stage III Exam

FLIGHT LESSON 15
DUAL — LOCAL (1.0)

NOTE: At the instructor's discretion, this lesson may be conducted at a nearby airport in the local area.

NOTE: A view-limiting device is required for the 0.5 hours of dual instrument time allocated to Flight Lesson 15.

OBJECTIVES
- Gain proficiency in using radio communications, navigation systems/facilities, and ATC services when flying solely by reference to instruments.
- Gain proficiency navigating with VOR, GPS, and ADF equipment.

PREFLIGHT DISCUSSION
- ❑ Navigation Equipment Limitations
- ❑ Operations in Turbulence
- ❑ Automation Management

REVIEW

NAVIGATION
❏ VOR Navigation
❏ GPS Navigation
❏ ADF Navigation, based on aircraft equipment
❏ Autopilot Use, if equipped

BASIC INSTRUMENT MANEUVERS
Control and maneuvering solely by reference to instruments
❏ Recovery from Unusual Flight Attitudes (IR)
❏ Using Radio Communications, Navigation Systems/Facilities, and ATC Services (IR)

TAKEOFFS, LANDINGS, AND GO-AROUNDS
❏ Short- and Soft-Field Takeoffs and Landings
❏ Normal and Crosswind Takeoffs and Landings

COMPLETION STANDARDS
• Recognize unusual flight attitudes solely by reference to instruments.
• Correctly apply the flight controls to recover from unusual attitudes while staying within the airplane's limitations.
• During flight solely by reference to instruments, maintain altitude ±250 feet, heading ±25°, and airspeed ±15 knots.
• Maintain the appropriate altitude, ±200 feet and heading ±15° while navigating with VOR, GPS, and ADF equipment.

POSTFLIGHT DEBRIEFING
❏ Critique maneuvers/procedures and SRM.
❏ Create a plan for skills that need improvement.
❏ Update the record folder and logbook.

STUDY ASSIGNMENT

Private Pilot Maneuvers Manual/e-Book
  Special Flight Operations: Night Operations

Maneuvers Lessons, Private Pilot Online — Jeppesen Learning Center
  ML18 — Night Operations

FLIGHT LESSON 16
DUAL — NIGHT LOCAL (1.0)

NOTE: *The 10 night takeoffs and landings to a full stop with each involving flight in the traffic pattern are an FAR Part 141 and 61 requirement. Five are scheduled for Flight Lesson 16 and the other five for Flight Lesson 18. However, this requirement may be accomplished with fewer than five during a flight, as long as the total of 10 is completed.*

STAGE II ■ **Flight Training Syllabus**

REFERENCES

Private Pilot Maneuvers Manual/e-Book
Special Flight Operations: Night Operations

Private Pilot Online — Jeppesen Learning Center
Maneuvers Lesson 18 — Night Operations

OBJECTIVES
- Become familiar with night operations, including night takeoffs, climbs, traffic patterns, approaches, and landings.
- Become familiar with the physiological factors and additional planning associated with the night environment.

PREFLIGHT DISCUSSION
- ❑ Aeromedical Factors
- ❑ CFIT Awareness and Wire Strike Avoidance
- ❑ Visual Illusions and Disorientation
- ❑ Night Vision and Night Scanning/Collision Avoidance
- ❑ Airplane Equipment and Lighting Requirements for Night Operation
- ❑ Airport and Obstruction Lighting
- ❑ Pilot-Controlled Lighting
- ❑ Personal Equipment

INTRODUCE

NIGHT OPERATIONS

PREFLIGHT PREPARATION—NIGHT
- ❑ Flight Planning for Night Operations
- ❑ Airworthiness Requirements
- ❑ Physiological Aspects of Night Flight—Vision

PREFLIGHT PROCEDURES—NIGHT
- ❑ Preflight Inspection
- ❑ Flight Deck Management
- ❑ Operation of Systems
- ❑ Use of Checklists
- ❑ Taxiing
- ❑ Before Takeoff Check/Runup

NIGHT CONSIDERATIONS
- ❑ Airport Lighting
- ❑ Collision Avoidance
- ❑ Night Orientation, Navigation, and Chart Reading

STALLS AND SLOW FLIGHT
Stall entries from various flight attitudes and power combinations with recovery initiated at the first indication of a stall, and recovery from a full stall

- ❑ Maneuvering During Slow Flight
- ❑ Power-Off Stalls
- ❑ Power-On Stalls
- ❑ Spin Awareness

PERFORMANCE MANEUVERS
- ❑ Steep Turns

TAKEOFFS, LANDINGS, AND GO-AROUNDS
- ❑ Short- and Soft-Field Takeoffs and Landings
- ❑ Normal and Crosswind Takeoffs and Landings
- ❑ Go-Around/Rejected Landing

COMPLETION STANDARDS
- Explain the night flight considerations, including vision limitations, collision avoidance, airport and airplane lighting, and navigation procedures.
- Maintain altitude ± 150 feet during level turns, straight-and-level flight, and slow flight. Stall recoveries should be coordinated with minimum altitude loss.
- Complete 5 takeoffs and landings to a full stop with each landing involving flight in the traffic pattern.
- Perform stabilized approaches to landing and touch down at a predetermined area on the runway.

POSTFLIGHT DEBRIEFING
- ❑ Critique maneuvers/procedures and SRM.
- ❑ Create a plan for skills that need improvement.
- ❑ Update the record folder and logbook.

STUDY ASSIGNMENT
Review, as required, in preparation for the dual cross-country in Flight Lesson 17.

FLIGHT LESSON 17
DUAL — CROSS-COUNTRY (2.0)

NOTE: A view-limiting device is required for the 0.5 hours of dual instrument time allocated to Flight Lesson 17.

NOTE: The flight must include a point of landing at a straight-line distance of more than 50 NM from the original point of departure.

OBJECTIVES
- Plan and implement a VFR cross-country flight that includes a point of landing at a straight-line distance of more than 50 NM from the original point of departure.
- Interpret aeronautical charts for VFR navigation using pilotage and dead reckoning with the aid of a magnetic compass.
- Use aircraft performance charts pertaining to cross-country flight.

STAGE II ■ **Flight Training Syllabus**

- Procure and analyze aeronautical weather reports and forecasts, including recognition of critical weather situations and estimating visibility while in flight.
- Recognize, avoid, and identify the operational restrictions of hazardous terrain features in the geographical area where the cross-country flight will be flown.
- Perform lost procedures and explain how to implement a diversion to an alternate airport.

PREFLIGHT DISCUSSION
❑ Hazardous Terrain—Recognition, Avoidance, and Operational Restrictions
❑ Airspace Requirements
❑ Temporary Flight Restrictions (TFRs)
❑ NOTAMs
❑ Weather Briefing

INTRODUCE

CROSS-COUNTRY FLIGHT PLANNING

PREFLIGHT PREPARATION
❑ Aeronautical Charts
❑ National Airspace System
❑ Flight Publications
❑ Route Selection
❑ Pilotage and Dead Reckoning
❑ Weather Information
❑ Weight and Balance
❑ Performance and Limitations
❑ Fuel Requirements
❑ Navigation Log
❑ Flight Plan
❑ Risk Management

CROSS-COUNTRY FLIGHT

CROSS-COUNTRY PROCEDURES
❑ Collision Avoidance
❑ Flight Deck Management
❑ Operation of Systems
❑ Power Settings and Mixture Control
❑ CFIT Avoidance
❑ Use of ATC Services
❑ Estimating Visibility in Flight
❑ Flight on Federal Airways
❑ Opening and Closing Flight Plan
❑ Single-Pilot Resource Management (SRM)
❑ Aeronautical Decision Making (ADM)
❑ Risk Management

NAVIGATION
❑ Course Interception

- ❑ Pilotage
- ❑ Dead Reckoning
- ❑ Estimating Groundspeed and ETA
- ❑ VOR, GPS, or ADF Navigation, based on aircraft equipment
- ❑ Position Fix by Navigation Facilities
- ❑ Lost Procedures
- ❑ Diversion
- ❑ Autopilot Use, if equipped

REVIEW

BASIC INSTRUMENT MANEUVERS
Control and maneuvering solely by reference to instruments
- ❑ Recovery from Unusual Flight Attitudes (IR)
- ❑ Using Radio Communications, Navigation Systems/Facilities, and ATC Services (IR)
- ❑ VOR, GPS, ADF Navigation (IR), based on aircraft equipment

EMERGENCY OPERATIONS
- ❑ Systems and Equipment Malfunctions
- ❑ Emergency Descent
- ❑ Emergency Approach and Landing (Simulated)
- ❑ Emergency Equipment and Survival Gear

AIRPORT OPERATIONS
- ❑ Airport, Runway, and Taxiway Signs, Markings, and Lighting
- ❑ Runway Incursion Avoidance
- ❑ Radio Communications
- ❑ Traffic Patterns/Departure, Arrival, Entry, and Approach Procedures
- ❑ Wake Turbulence Avoidance
- ❑ Wind Shear Avoidance

COMPLETION STANDARDS:
- Plan and conduct a cross-country flight, including weather analysis, use of flight publications and aeronautical charts, adherence to the preflight plan, and navigation through the use of pilotage, dead reckoning, radio communication, and navigation systems.
- Determine location at any time and compute ETAs within 10 minutes.
- Determine the aircraft position during lost procedures.
- Given a scenario, make a timely decision to divert and select a suitable airport and route for diversion.
- Complete at least one landing at a point that is a straight-line distance of more than 50 NM from the original point of departure.

POSTFLIGHT DEBRIEFING
- ❑ Critique maneuvers/procedures and SRM.
- ❑ Create a plan for skills that need improvement.
- ❑ Update the record folder and logbook.

FLIGHT LESSON 18
DUAL — NIGHT CROSS-COUNTRY (2.0)

NOTE: A view-limiting device is required for the 0.5 hours of dual instrument time allocated to Flight Lesson 18.

NOTE: The flight must include a total distance of more than 100 NM and a point of landing at a straight-line distance of more than 50 NM from the original point of departure.

OBJECTIVES
- Perform effective flight planning considering the night environment.
- Fly the mission with precise aircraft control and navigate with the accuracy required to successfully complete a night VFR cross-country flight.

PREFLIGHT DISCUSSION
❑ Night Orientation, Navigation, and Chart Reading Techniques
❑ Hazardous Terrain—Recognition, Avoidance, and Operational Restrictions
❑ Airspace Requirements
❑ Temporary Flight Restrictions (TFRs)
❑ NOTAMs
❑ Weather Briefing

INTRODUCE

CROSS-COUNTRY FLIGHT PLANNING

PREFLIGHT PREPARATION—NIGHT
❑ Aeronautical Charts
❑ National Airspace System
❑ Flight Publications
❑ Route Selection
❑ Pilotage and Dead Reckoning
❑ Weather Information
❑ Weight and Balance
❑ Performance and Limitations
❑ Fuel Requirements
❑ Navigation Log
❑ FAA Flight Plan
❑ Risk Management
❑ Flight Planning Considerations—Night
❑ Physiological Aspects of Night Flight—Vision

CROSS-COUNTRY FLIGHT

CROSS-COUNTRY PROCEDURES
❑ Collision Avoidance
❑ Flight Deck Management
❑ Operation of Systems
❑ Power Settings and Mixture Control

- ❏ CFIT Avoidance
- ❏ Use of ATC Services
- ❏ Estimating Visibility in Flight
- ❏ Lost Procedures
- ❏ Diversion
- ❏ Flight on Federal Airways
- ❏ Opening and Closing Flight Plan
- ❏ Single-Pilot Resource Management (SRM)
- ❏ Aeronautical Decision Making (ADM)
- ❏ Risk Management

NAVIGATION
- ❏ Course Interception
- ❏ Pilotage
- ❏ Dead Reckoning
- ❏ Estimating of Groundspeed and ETA
- ❏ VOR, GPS, or ADF Navigation, based on aircraft equipment
- ❏ Position Fix by Navigation Facilities
- ❏ Autopilot Use, if equipped

REVIEW

BASIC INSTRUMENT MANEUVERS
Control and maneuvering solely by reference to instruments
- ❏ Recovery from Unusual Flight Attitudes (IR)
- ❏ Using Radio Communications, Navigation Systems/Facilities, and ATC Services (IR)
- ❏ VOR, GPS, ADF Navigation (IR), based on aircraft equipment

EMERGENCY OPERATIONS
- ❏ Systems and Equipment Malfunctions
- ❏ Emergency Descent
- ❏ Emergency Approach and Landing (Simulated)
- ❏ Emergency Equipment and Survival Gear

AIRPORT OPERATIONS
- ❏ Airport, Runway, and Taxiway Signs, Markings, and Lighting
- ❏ Runway Incursion Avoidance
- ❏ Radio Communications
- ❏ Traffic Patterns/Departure, Arrival, Entry, and Approach Procedures
- ❏ Wake Turbulence Avoidance
- ❏ Wind Shear Avoidance

COMPLETION STANDARDS
- Demonstrate effective night cross-country preparation and flight procedures.
- Navigate accurately and handle simulated emergency situations promptly, utilizing good judgment.

STAGE II ■ Flight Training Syllabus

- Complete 5 takeoffs and landings to a full stop with each involving flight in the traffic pattern with one at least one landing at a point that is a straight-line distance of more than 50 NM from the original point of departure.
- Perform stabilized approaches to landing and touch down at a predetermined area on the runway.

POSTFLIGHT DEBRIEFING
❑ Critique maneuvers/procedures and SRM.
❑ Create a plan for skills that need improvement.
❑ Update the record folder and logbook.

STUDY ASSIGNMENT
Prepare for the Solo Cross-Country Briefing. (Refer to questions in Appendix A.)

FLIGHT LESSON 19
SOLO — CROSS-COUNTRY (2.5)

NOTE: This flight should include a point of landing that is at a straight-line distance of more than 50 NM from the original point of departure.

NOTE: Solo Cross-Country Briefing questions are included in Appendix A.

OBJECTIVES
- Complete the Solo Cross-Country Briefing.
- Plan and fly a solo cross-country flight.
- Determine alternatives if the flight cannot be completed as planned.
- Increase proficiency and confidence in solo and cross-country operations.

PREFLIGHT DISCUSSION
❑ Solo Cross-Country Briefing Review
❑ Required Documents and Endorsements
❑ Hazardous Terrain—Recognition, Avoidance, and Operational Restrictions
❑ Airspace Requirements
❑ Temporary Flight Restrictions (TFRs)
❑ NOTAMs
❑ Weather Briefing
❑ Lost Procedures
❑ Diversion
❑ Lost Communication Procedures
❑ Emergency Operations

REVIEW

CROSS-COUNTRY FLIGHT PLANNING

PREFLIGHT PREPARATION
❑ Aeronautical Charts
❑ National Airspace System

- ❏ Flight Publications
- ❏ Route Selection
- ❏ Pilotage and Dead Reckoning
- ❏ Weather Information
- ❏ Weight and Balance
- ❏ Performance and Limitations
- ❏ Fuel Requirements
- ❏ Navigation Log
- ❏ Flight Plan
- ❏ Risk Management

CROSS-COUNTRY FLIGHT

CROSS-COUNTRY PROCEDURES
- ❏ Collision Avoidance
- ❏ Flight Deck Management
- ❏ Operation of Systems
- ❏ CFIT Avoidance
- ❏ Use of ATC Services
- ❏ Power Settings and Mixture Control
- ❏ Estimating Visibility in Flight
- ❏ Flight on Federal Airways
- ❏ Opening and Closing Flight Plan
- ❏ Single-Pilot Resource Management (SRM)
- ❏ Aeronautical Decision Making (ADM)
- ❏ Risk Management

NAVIGATION
- ❏ Course Interception
- ❏ Pilotage
- ❏ Dead Reckoning
- ❏ Estimating Groundspeed and ETA
- ❏ VOR, GPS, or ADF Navigation, based on aircraft equipment
- ❏ Position Fix by Navigation Facilities
- ❏ Autopilot Use, if equipped

AIRPORT OPERATIONS
- ❏ Airport, Runway, and Taxiway Signs, Markings, and Lighting
- ❏ Runway Incursion Avoidance
- ❏ Radio Communications
- ❏ Traffic Patterns/Departure, Arrival, Entry, and Approach Procedures

COMPLETION STANDARDS
- Accurately plan and perform a solo VFR cross-country flight.
- Perform proper traffic pattern, departure, arrival, entry, and approach procedures at unfamiliar airports.
- Perform at least one landing more than 50 NM from the departure airport.

STAGE II ■ **Flight Training Syllabus**

POSTFLIGHT DEBRIEFING
❑ Critique maneuvers/procedures and SRM.
❑ Create a plan for skills that need improvement.
❑ Update the record folder and logbook.

STUDY ASSIGNMENT

Ground Lessons 16 and 17
 Final Exams A and B

Review as required in preparation for the Stage II Check in Flight Lesson 20.

FLIGHT LESSON 20
DUAL — LOCAL (1.0)
STAGE II CHECK

OBJECTIVES
Demonstrate to the chief instructor, the assistant chief instructor, or the designated check instructor:
- Proficiency in conducting takeoffs, landings, and stall recognition and recovery procedures.
- The ability to plan and conduct a cross-country flight, as well as safe and effective operation of the aircraft during all other phases of flight.

PREFLIGHT DISCUSSION
Conduct of the Stage II Check, including:
❑ Maneuvers and Procedures
❑ Acceptable Performance Criteria
❑ Applicable Rules

EVALUATE

CROSS-COUNTRY FLIGHT PLANNING

PREFLIGHT PREPARATION
❑ Aeronautical Charts
❑ National Airspace System
❑ Flight Publications
❑ Route Selection
❑ Pilotage and Dead Reckoning
❑ Weather Information
❑ Weight and Balance
❑ Performance and Limitations
❑ Fuel Requirements
❑ Navigation Log
❑ Flight Plan
❑ Risk Management

CROSS-COUNTRY FLIGHT

CROSS-COUNTRY PROCEDURES
- ❏ Collision Avoidance
- ❏ Flight Deck Management
- ❏ Operation of Systems
- ❏ Power Settings and Mixture Control
- ❏ CFIT Avoidance
- ❏ Use of ATC Services
- ❏ Estimating Visibility in Flight
- ❏ Flight on Federal Airways
- ❏ Opening and Closing Flight Plan

NAVIGATION
- ❏ Course Interception
- ❏ Pilotage
- ❏ Dead Reckoning
- ❏ Estimating Groundspeed and ETA
- ❏ VOR, GPS, or ADF Navigation, based on aircraft equipment
- ❏ Position Fix by Navigation Facilities
- ❏ Lost Procedures
- ❏ Diversion
- ❏ Autopilot Use, if equipped

BASIC INSTRUMENT MANEUVERS

Control and maneuvering solely by reference to instruments
- ❏ Recovery from Unusual Flight Attitudes (IR)
- ❏ Using Radio Communications, Navigation Systems/Facilities, and ATC Services (IR)
- ❏ VOR, GPS, ADF Navigation (IR), based on aircraft equipment

EMERGENCY OPERATIONS
- ❏ Systems and Equipment Malfunctions
- ❏ Emergency Descent
- ❏ Emergency Approach and Landing (Simulated)
- ❏ Emergency Equipment and Survival Gear

AIRPORT OPERATIONS
- ❏ Airport, Runway, and Taxiway Signs, Markings, and Lighting
- ❏ Runway Incursion Avoidance
- ❏ Radio Communications
- ❏ Traffic Patterns/Departure, Arrival, Entry, and Approach Procedures
- ❏ Wake Turbulence Avoidance
- ❏ Wind Shear Avoidance

TAKEOFFS, LANDINGS, AND GO-AROUNDS
- ❏ Normal and Crosswind Takeoffs and Landings
- ❏ Short- and Soft-Field Takeoffs and Landings

STAGE II ■ **Flight Training Syllabus**

COMPLETION STANDARDS

- Plan and conduct a cross-country flight, including weather analysis, use of flight publications and aeronautical charts, adherence to the preflight plan, and navigation through the use of pilotage, dead reckoning, radio communication, and navigation systems.
- Determine location at any time and compute ETAs within 10 minutes.
- Determine the aircraft position during lost procedures.
- Given a scenario, make a timely decision to divert and select a suitable airport and route for diversion.

POSTFLIGHT DEBRIEFING

- ❑ Evaluate maneuvers/procedures and SRM.
- ❑ Plan further instruction for skills not meeting Stage II completion standards.
- ❑ Update the record folder and logbook.

STAGE II ■ **Flight Training Syllabus**

Stage III

STAGE OBJECTIVES
During this stage, the student will gain additional proficiency in solo cross-country operations and will receive instruction in preparation for the End-of-Course Flight Check.

STAGE COMPLETION STANDARDS
This stage will be complete when the student demonstrates performance of private pilot operations at a standard that meets or exceeds the minimum performance criteria established in the FAA *Private Pilot — Airplane Airman Certification Standards*.

FLIGHT LESSON 21
SOLO — CROSS-COUNTRY (2.0)

NOTE: The flight must include a point of landing at a straight-line distance of more than 50 NM from the original point of departure.

NOTE: The flight should include three takeoffs and landings to a full stop with each landing involving flight in the traffic pattern at an airport with an operating control tower. However, at the instructor's discretion, this solo training requirement may be completed in other flight lessons.

OBJECTIVES
* Complete the scheduled cross-country flight to improve judgment and confidence when operating in unfamiliar areas.
* Competently execute cross-country procedures and comply with rules for flight within Class D airspace.

PREFLIGHT DISCUSSION
❑ Solo Cross-Country Briefing Review
❑ Required Documents and Endorsements
❑ Hazardous Terrain—Recognition, Avoidance, and Operational Restrictions
❑ Airspace Requirements
❑ Temporary Flight Restrictions (TFRs)
❑ NOTAMs
❑ Weather Briefing
❑ Lost Procedures
❑ Diversion
❑ Lost Communication Procedures
❑ Emergency Operations

REVIEW

CROSS-COUNTRY FLIGHT PLANNING

PREFLIGHT PREPARATION
❏ Aeronautical Charts
❏ National Airspace System
❏ Flight Publications
❏ Route Selection
❏ Pilotage and Dead Reckoning
❏ Weather Information
❏ Weight and Balance
❏ Performance and Limitations
❏ Fuel Requirements
❏ Navigation Log
❏ Flight Plan
❏ Risk Management

CROSS-COUNTRY FLIGHT

CROSS-COUNTRY PROCEDURES
❏ Collision Avoidance
❏ Flight Deck Management
❏ Operation of Systems
❏ Power Settings and Mixture Control
❏ CFIT Avoidance
❏ Use of ATC Services
❏ Estimating Visibility in Flight
❏ Flight on Federal Airways
❏ Opening and Closing the Flight Plan
❏ Single-Pilot Resource Management (SRM)
❏ Aeronautical Decision Making (ADM)
❏ Risk Management

NAVIGATION
❏ Course Interception
❏ Pilotage
❏ Dead Reckoning
❏ Estimating Groundspeed and ETA
❏ VOR, GPS, ADF Navigation, based on aircraft equipment
❏ Autopilot Use, if equipped

AIRPORT OPERATIONS
❏ Airport, Runway, and Taxiway Signs, Markings, and Lighting
❏ Runway Incursion Avoidance
❏ Radio Communications
❏ Traffic Patterns/Departure, Arrival, Entry, and Approach Procedures

COMPLETION STANDARDS
- Accurately plan and perform a solo VFR cross-country flight.
- Perform proper traffic pattern, departure, arrival, entry, and approach procedures at unfamiliar airports.
- Perform at least one landing more than 50 NM from the departure airport.
- Complete three takeoffs and landings, with flight in the traffic pattern, at a controlled airport.

POSTFLIGHT DEBRIEFING
- ❑ Critique maneuvers/procedures and SRM.
- ❑ Create a plan for skills that need improvement.
- ❑ Update the record folder and logbook.

FLIGHT LESSON 22
SOLO — CROSS-COUNTRY (4.0)

NOTE: Due to the amount of time needed to complete this cross-country flight, the lesson may be conducted as two flights. If this is done, and in order for the flight to be classified as cross-country, each flight must include a landing more than 50 NM from the departure airport.

NOTE: The flight should include three takeoffs and landings to a full stop with each landing involving flight in the traffic pattern at an airport with an operating control tower. However, at the instructor's discretion, this solo training requirement may be completed in other flight lessons.

OBJECTIVES
- Complete the long cross-country flight requirement, which includes a flight with a total distance of at least 100 NM, with landings at a minimum of three points, including a straight-line segment more than 50 NM between takeoff and landing locations.
- Competently execute cross-country procedures and comply with rules for flight within Class D airspace.

PREFLIGHT DISCUSSION
- ❑ Solo Cross-Country Briefing Review
- ❑ Required Documents and Endorsements
- ❑ Hazardous Terrain—Recognition, Avoidance, and Operational Restrictions
- ❑ Airspace Requirements
- ❑ Temporary Flight Restrictions (TFRs)
- ❑ NOTAMs
- ❑ Weather Briefing
- ❑ Lost Procedures
- ❑ Diversion
- ❑ Lost Communication Procedures
- ❑ Emergency Operations

STAGE III ■ Flight Training Syllabus

REVIEW

CROSS-COUNTRY FLIGHT PLANNING

PREFLIGHT PREPARATION
❑ Aeronautical Charts
❑ National Airspace System
❑ Flight Publications
❑ Route Selection
❑ Pilotage and Dead Reckoning
❑ Weather Information
❑ Weight and Balance
❑ Performance and Limitations
❑ Fuel Requirements
❑ Navigation Log
❑ Flight Plan
❑ Risk Management

CROSS-COUNTRY FLIGHT

CROSS-COUNTRY PROCEDURES
❑ Collision Avoidance
❑ Flight Deck Management
❑ Operation of Systems
❑ Power Settings and Mixture Control
❑ CFIT Avoidance
❑ Use of ATC Services
❑ Estimating Visibility in Flight
❑ Flight on Federal Airways
❑ Opening and Closing the Flight Plan
❑ Single-Pilot Resource Management (SRM)
❑ Aeronautical Decision Making (ADM)
❑ Risk Management

NAVIGATION
❑ Course Interception
❑ Pilotage
❑ Dead Reckoning
❑ Estimating Groundspeed and ETA
❑ VOR, GPS, ADF Navigation, based on aircraft equipment
❑ Autopilot Use, if equipped

AIRPORT OPERATIONS
❑ Airport, Runway, and Taxiway Signs, Markings, and Lighting
❑ Runway Incursion Avoidance
❑ Radio Communications
❑ Traffic Patterns/Departure, Arrival, Entry, and Approach Procedures

STAGE III ■ **Flight Training Syllabus**

COMPLETION STANDARDS
- Accurately plan and perform a solo VFR cross-country flight.
- Perform proper traffic pattern, departure, arrival, entry, and approach procedures at unfamiliar airports.
- Perform at least one landing more than 50 NM from the departure airport.
- Complete three takeoffs and landings, with flight in the traffic pattern, at a controlled airport.

POSTFLIGHT DEBRIEFING
- ❑ Critique maneuvers/procedures and SRM.
- ❑ Create a plan for skills that need improvement.
- ❑ Update the record folder and logbook.

FLIGHT LESSON 22
SOLO — CROSS-COUNTRY (4.0)

NOTE: Due to the amount of time needed to complete this cross-country flight, the lesson may be conducted as two flights. If this is done, and in order for the flight to be classified as cross-country, each flight must include a landing more than 50 NM from the departure airport.

NOTE: The flight should include three takeoffs and landings to a full stop with each landing involving flight in the traffic pattern at an airport with an operating control tower. However, at the instructor's discretion, this solo training requirement may be completed in other flight lessons.

OBJECTIVES
- Complete the long cross-country flight requirement, which includes a flight of at least 100 NM total distance, with landings at a minimum of three points, including a straight-line segment more than 50 NM between takeoff and landing locations.
- Competently execute cross-country procedures and comply with rules for flight within Class D airspace.

PREFLIGHT DISCUSSION
- ❑ Solo Cross-Country Briefing Review
- ❑ Required Documents and Endorsements
- ❑ Hazardous Terrain—Recognition, Avoidance, and Operational Restrictions
- ❑ Airspace Requirements
- ❑ Temporary Flight Restrictions (TFRs)
- ❑ NOTAMs
- ❑ Weather Briefing
- ❑ Lost Procedures
- ❑ Diversion
- ❑ Lost Communication Procedures
- ❑ Emergency Operations

STAGE III ■ Flight Training Syllabus

REVIEW

CROSS-COUNTRY FLIGHT PLANNING

PREFLIGHT PREPARATION
- ❏ Aeronautical Charts
- ❏ National Airspace System
- ❏ Flight Publications
- ❏ Route Selection
- ❏ Pilotage and Dead Reckoning
- ❏ Weather Information
- ❏ Weight and Balance
- ❏ Performance and Limitations
- ❏ Fuel Requirements
- ❏ Navigation Log
- ❏ Flight Plan
- ❏ Risk Management

CROSS-COUNTRY FLIGHT

CROSS-COUNTRY PROCEDURES
- ❏ Collision Avoidance
- ❏ Flight Deck Management
- ❏ Operation of Systems
- ❏ Power Settings and Mixture Control
- ❏ CFIT Avoidance
- ❏ Use of ATC Services
- ❏ Estimating Visibility in Flight
- ❏ Flight on Federal Airways
- ❏ Opening and Closing the Flight Plan
- ❏ Single-Pilot Resource Management (SRM)

NAVIGATION
- ❏ Course Interception
- ❏ Pilotage
- ❏ Dead Reckoning
- ❏ Estimating Groundspeed and ETA
- ❏ VOR, GPS, ADF Navigation, based on aircraft equipment
- ❏ Autopilot Use, if equipped

AIRPORT OPERATIONS
- ❏ Airport, Runway, and Taxiway Signs, Markings, and Lighting
- ❏ Runway Incursion Avoidance
- ❏ Radio Communications
- ❏ Traffic Patterns/Departure, Arrival, Entry, and Approach Procedures

COMPLETION STANDARDS
- Accurately plan and perform a solo VFR cross-country flight of over 100 NM with landings at a minimum of three points, including at least one segment of the flight consisting of straight-line distance of more than 50 NM between takeoff and landing locations.
- Perform proper traffic pattern, departure, arrival, entry, and approach procedures at unfamiliar airports.
- Complete three takeoffs and landings, with flight in the traffic pattern, at a controlled airport (if not completed on previous solo flights).

POSTFLIGHT DEBRIEFING
❑ Critique maneuvers/procedures and SRM.
❑ Create a plan for skills that need improvement.
❑ Update the record folder and logbook.

FLIGHT LESSON 23
DUAL — LOCAL (2.0)

OBJECTIVES
- Review the areas of operation, including specified maneuvers and procedures assigned by the instructor to increase proficiency to the level required of a private pilot.
- Gain additional knowledge and skill in preparation for the private pilot practical test.
- Correct any deficient skill and knowledge areas.

PREFLIGHT DISCUSSION
❑ Maneuvers and Procedures in Preparation for the Stage III Check, End-of-Course Flight Check, and FAA Private Pilot Practical Test
❑ Spin Awareness and Night Operations
❑ Private Pilot Airman Certification Standards

REVIEW

PREFLIGHT PREPARATION
❑ Pilot Qualifications
❑ Airworthiness Requirements
❑ Weather Information
❑ Cross-Country Flight Planning
❑ National Airspace System
❑ Performance and Limitations
❑ Operation of Systems
❑ Human Factors

STAGE III ■ **Flight Training Syllabus**

PREFLIGHT PROCEDURES
❑ Self-Assessment
❑ Preflight Inspection
❑ Passenger Briefing
❑ Flight Deck Management
❑ Operation of Systems
❑ Use of Checklists
❑ Engine Starting
❑ Taxiing
❑ Before Takeoff Check/Runup

AIRPORT OPERATIONS
❑ Airport Security
❑ Airport, Runway, and Taxiway Signs, Markings, and Lighting
❑ Runway Incursion Avoidance
❑ Radio Communications
❑ Traffic Patterns/Departure, Arrival, Entry, and Approach Procedures
❑ Lost Communication Procedures/ATC Light Signals
❑ Wake Turbulence Avoidance
❑ Wind Shear Avoidance

SLOW FLIGHT AND STALLS
Stall entries from various flight attitudes and power combinations with recovery initiated at the first indication of a stall, and recovery from a full stall
❑ Maneuvering During Slow Flight
❑ Power-Off Stalls
❑ Power-On Stalls
❑ Spin Awareness

PERFORMANCE MANEUVERS
❑ Steep Turns

GROUND REFERENCE MANEUVERS
❑ Rectangular Courses
❑ S-Turns
❑ Turns Around a Point

TAKEOFFS, LANDINGS, AND GO-AROUNDS
❑ Takeoff Briefing
❑ Before Landing Briefing
❑ Rejected Takeoff
❑ Go-Around/Rejected Landing
❑ Forward Slip to a Landing
❑ Normal and Crosswind Takeoffs and Landings
❑ Short- and Soft-Field Takeoffs and Landings

NAVIGATION
- ❑ Course Interception
- ❑ Pilotage
- ❑ Dead Reckoning
- ❑ Estimating Groundspeed and ETA
- ❑ VOR, GPS, or ADF Navigation (VR/IR), based on aircraft equipment
- ❑ Position Fix by Navigation Facilities
- ❑ Lost Procedures
- ❑ Diversion
- ❑ Autopilot Use, if equipped

BASIC INSTRUMENT MANEUVERS
Control and maneuvering solely by reference to instruments
- ❑ Straight-and-Level Flight (IR)
- ❑ Constant Airspeed Climbs (IR)
- ❑ Constant Airspeed Descents (IR)
- ❑ Turns to Headings (IR)
- ❑ Recovery from Unusual Flight Attitudes (IR)
- ❑ Using Radio Communications, Navigation Systems/Facilities, and ATC Services (IR)

EMERGENCY OPERATIONS
- ❑ Systems and Equipment Malfunctions
- ❑ Emergency Descent
- ❑ Emergency Approach and Landing (Simulated)
- ❑ Emergency Equipment and Survival Gear

POSTFLIGHT PROCEDURES
- ❑ After Landing, Parking, and Securing

COMPLETION STANDARDS
- Demonstrate satisfactory knowledge, risk management, and skills associated with all maneuvers and procedures required by the Private Pilot Airman Certification Standards.
- Demonstrate proficiency in performing each assigned maneuver according to the criteria established by the Private Pilot Airman Certification Standards.

POSTFLIGHT DEBRIEFING
- ❑ Critique maneuvers/procedures and SRM.
- ❑ Create a plan for skills that need improvement.
- ❑ Update the record folder and logbook.

STAGE III ■ **Flight Training Syllabus**

FLIGHT LESSON 24
DUAL — LOCAL (2.0)

OBJECTIVES
- Review the areas of operation, including specified maneuvers and procedures assigned by the instructor to increase proficiency to the level required of a private pilot.
- Gain additional knowledge and skill in preparation for the private pilot practical test.
- Correct any deficient skill and knowledge areas.

PREFLIGHT DISCUSSION
❑ Maneuvers and Procedures in Preparation for the Stage III Check, End-of-Course Flight Check, and FAA Private Pilot Practical Test
❑ Spin Awareness and Night Operations
❑ Private Pilot Airman Certification Standards

REVIEW

PREFLIGHT PREPARATION
❑ Pilot Qualifications
❑ Airworthiness Requirements
❑ Weather Information
❑ Cross-Country Flight Planning
❑ National Airspace System
❑ Performance and Limitations
❑ Operation of Systems
❑ Human Factors

PREFLIGHT PROCEDURES
❑ Self-Assessment
❑ Preflight Inspection
❑ Passenger Briefing
❑ Flight Deck Management
❑ Operation of Systems
❑ Use of Checklists
❑ Engine Starting
❑ Taxiing
❑ Before Takeoff Check/Runup

Private Pilot Syllabus

AIRPORT OPERATIONS
- ❑ Airport Security
- ❑ Airport, Runway, and Taxiway Signs, Markings, and Lighting
- ❑ Runway Incursion Avoidance
- ❑ Radio Communications
- ❑ Traffic Patterns/Departure, Arrival, Entry, and Approach Procedures
- ❑ Lost Communication Procedures/ATC Light Signals
- ❑ Wake Turbulence Avoidance
- ❑ Wind Shear Avoidance

SLOW FLIGHT AND STALLS
Stall entries from various flight attitudes and power combinations with recovery initiated at the first indication of a stall, and recovery from a full stall
- ❑ Maneuvering During Slow Flight
- ❑ Power-Off Stalls
- ❑ Power-On Stalls
- ❑ Spin Awareness

PERFORMANCE MANEUVERS
- ❑ Steep Turns

GROUND REFERENCE MANEUVERS
- ❑ Rectangular Courses
- ❑ S-Turns
- ❑ Turns Around a Point

NAVIGATION
- ❑ Course Interception
- ❑ Pilotage
- ❑ Dead Reckoning
- ❑ Estimating Groundspeed and ETA
- ❑ VOR, GPS, or ADF Navigation (VR/IR), based on aircraft equipment
- ❑ Position Fix by Navigation Facilities
- ❑ Lost Procedures
- ❑ Diversion
- ❑ Autopilot Use, if equipped

BASIC INSTRUMENT MANEUVERS
Control and maneuvering solely by reference to instruments
- ❑ Straight-and-Level Flight (IR)
- ❑ Constant Airspeed Climbs (IR)
- ❑ Constant Airspeed Descents (IR)
- ❑ Turns to Headings (IR)
- ❑ Recovery from Unusual Flight Attitudes (IR)
- ❑ Using Radio Communications, Navigation Systems/Facilities, and ATC Services (IR)

STAGE III ■ **Flight Training Syllabus**

EMERGENCY OPERATIONS
- ❏ Systems and Equipment Malfunctions
- ❏ Emergency Descent
- ❏ Emergency Approach and Landing (Simulated)
- ❏ Emergency Equipment and Survival Gear

TAKEOFFS, LANDINGS, AND GO-AROUNDS
- ❏ Takeoff Briefing
- ❏ Before Landing Briefing
- ❏ Rejected Takeoff
- ❏ Go-Around/Rejected Landing
- ❏ Forward Slip to a Landing
- ❏ Normal and Crosswind Takeoffs and Landings
- ❏ Short- and Soft-Field Takeoffs and Landings

POSTFLIGHT PROCEDURES
- ❏ After Landing, Parking, and Securing

COMPLETION STANDARDS
- Correct any weak performance areas determined previously.
- Demonstrate satisfactory knowledge, risk management, and skills associated with all maneuvers and procedures required by the Private Pilot Airman Certification Standards.
- Demonstrate proficiency in performing each assigned maneuver according to the criteria established by the Private Pilot Airman Certification Standards.

POSTFLIGHT DEBRIEFING
- ❏ Critique maneuvers/procedures and SRM.
- ❏ Create a plan for skills that need improvement.
- ❏ Update the record folder and logbook.

FLIGHT LESSON 25
DUAL — LOCAL (1.0)

STAGE III CHECK

OBJECTIVES
Demonstrate to the chief instructor, the assistant chief instructor, or the designated check instructor:
- Satisfactory knowledge, risk management, and skills associated with all maneuvers and procedures required by the Private Pilot Airman Certification Standards.
- Proficiency in performing each assigned maneuver according to the criteria established by the Private Pilot Airman Certification Standards.
- Single-pilot resource management (SRM) skills, including aeronautical decision-making (ADM), and risk management.

PREFLIGHT DISCUSSION

Conduct of the Stage III Check, including:

❑ Maneuvers and Procedures
❑ Acceptable Performance Criteria
❑ Applicable Rules
❑ Human Factors Concepts

EVALUATE

PREFLIGHT PREPARATION

❑ Pilot Qualifications
❑ Airworthiness Requirements
❑ Weather Information
❑ Cross-Country Flight Planning
❑ National Airspace System
❑ Performance and Limitations
❑ Operation of Systems
❑ Human Factors

PREFLIGHT PROCEDURES

❑ Self-Assessment
❑ Preflight Inspection
❑ Passenger Briefing
❑ Flight Deck Management
❑ Operation of Systems
❑ Use of Checklists
❑ Engine Starting
❑ Taxiing
❑ Before Takeoff Check/Runup

AIRPORT OPERATIONS

❑ Airport Security
❑ Airport, Runway, and Taxiway Signs, Markings, and Lighting
❑ Runway Incursion Avoidance
❑ Radio Communications
❑ Traffic Patterns/Departure, Arrival, Entry, and Approach Procedures
❑ Lost Communication Procedures/ATC Light Signals
❑ Wake Turbulence Avoidance
❑ Wind Shear Avoidance

STAGE III ■ **Flight Training Syllabus**

SLOW FLIGHT AND STALLS
Stall entries from various flight attitudes and power combinations with recovery initiated at the first indication of a stall, and recovery from a full stall
- ❑ Maneuvering During Slow Flight
- ❑ Power-Off Stalls
- ❑ Power-On Stalls
- ❑ Spin Awareness

PERFORMANCE MANEUVERS
- ❑ Steep Turns

GROUND REFERENCE MANEUVERS
- ❑ Rectangular Courses
- ❑ S-Turns
- ❑ Turns Around a Point

NAVIGATION
- ❑ Course Interception
- ❑ Pilotage
- ❑ Dead Reckoning
- ❑ Estimating Groundspeed and ETA
- ❑ VOR, GPS, or ADF Navigation (VR/IR), based on aircraft equipment
- ❑ Position Fix by Navigation Facilities
- ❑ Lost Procedures
- ❑ Diversion
- ❑ Autopilot Use, if equipped

BASIC INSTRUMENT MANEUVERS
Control and maneuvering solely by reference to instruments
- ❑ Straight-and-Level Flight (IR)
- ❑ Constant Airspeed Climbs (IR)
- ❑ Constant Airspeed Descents (IR)
- ❑ Turns to Headings (IR)
- ❑ Recovery from Unusual Flight Attitudes (IR)
- ❑ Using Radio Communications, Navigation Systems/Facilities, and ATC Services (IR)

EMERGENCY OPERATIONS
- ❑ Systems and Equipment Malfunctions
- ❑ Emergency Descent
- ❑ Emergency Approach and Landing (Simulated)
- ❑ Emergency Equipment and Survival Gear

TAKEOFFS, LANDINGS, AND GO-AROUNDS
❏ Takeoff Briefing
❏ Before Landing Briefing
❏ Rejected Takeoff
❏ Go-Around/Rejected Landing
❏ Forward Slip to a Landing
❏ Normal and Crosswind Takeoffs and Landings
❏ Short- and Soft-Field Takeoffs and Landings

POSTFLIGHT PROCEDURES
❏ After Landing, Parking, and Securing

COMPLETION STANDARDS
- Demonstrate satisfactory knowledge, risk management, and skills associated with all maneuvers and procedures required by the Private Pilot Airman Certification Standards.
- Demonstrate proficiency in performing each assigned maneuver according to the criteria established by the Private Pilot Airman Certification Standards.
- Demonstrate single-pilot resource management (SRM) skills, including aeronautical decision-making (ADM), and risk management.
- Demonstrate mastery of the airplane so that the successful outcome of each task performed is never in doubt.
- Demonstrate sound understanding of the knowledge, skill, and proficiency requirements for private pilot certification.

POSTFLIGHT DEBRIEFING
❏ Critique maneuvers/procedures and SRM.
❏ Plan further instruction for skills not meeting Stage III completion standards.
❏ Update the record folder and logbook.

Any maneuvers or procedures that do not meet private pilot standards should be reviewed with the student and assigned additional practice.

STUDY ASSIGNMENT
Complete the Private Pilot Practical Test Briefing with the instructor in preparation for the End-of-Course Flight Check and the FAA Private Pilot Practical Test. Suggested questions for this briefing are included in Appendix A.

STAGE III ■ **Flight Training Syllabus**

FLIGHT LESSON 26
DUAL — LOCAL (1.0)
END-OF-COURSE FLIGHT CHECK

OBJECTIVES
Demonstrate to the chief instructor, the assistant chief instructor, or the designated check instructor:
- Satisfactory knowledge, risk management, and skills associated with all maneuvers and procedures required by the Private Pilot Airman Certification Standards.
- Proficiency in performing each assigned maneuver according to the criteria established by the Private Pilot Airman Certification Standards.
- Single-pilot resource management (SRM) skills, including aeronautical decision-making (ADM), and risk management.

PREFLIGHT DISCUSSION
Conduct of the End-of-Course Flight Check, Including:
- ❏ Maneuvers
- ❏ Procedures
- ❏ Acceptable Performance Criteria
- ❏ Applicable Rules

EVALUATE

PREFLIGHT PREPARATION
- ❏ Pilot Qualifications
- ❏ Airworthiness Requirements
- ❏ Weather Information
- ❏ Cross-Country Flight Planning
- ❏ National Airspace System
- ❏ Performance and Limitations
- ❏ Operation of Systems
- ❏ Human Factors

PREFLIGHT PROCEDURES
- ❏ Self-Assessment
- ❏ Preflight Inspection
- ❏ Passenger Briefing
- ❏ Flight Deck Management
- ❏ Operation of Systems
- ❏ Use of Checklists
- ❏ Engine Starting
- ❏ Taxiing
- ❏ Before Takeoff Check/Runup

AIRPORT OPERATIONS
- ❑ Airport Security
- ❑ Airport, Runway, and Taxiway Signs, Markings, and Lighting
- ❑ Runway Incursion Avoidance
- ❑ Radio Communications
- ❑ Traffic Patterns/Departure, Arrival, Entry, and Approach Procedures
- ❑ Lost Communication Procedures/ATC Light Signals
- ❑ Wake Turbulence Avoidance
- ❑ Wind Shear Avoidance

SLOW FLIGHT AND STALLS
Stall entries from various flight attitudes and power combinations with recovery initiated at the first indication of a stall, and recovery from a full stall
- ❑ Maneuvering During Slow Flight
- ❑ Power-Off Stalls
- ❑ Power-On Stalls
- ❑ Spin Awareness

PERFORMANCE MANEUVERS
- ❑ Steep Turns

GROUND REFERENCE MANEUVERS
- ❑ Rectangular Courses
- ❑ S-Turns
- ❑ Turns Around a Point

NAVIGATION
- ❑ Course Interception
- ❑ Pilotage
- ❑ Dead Reckoning
- ❑ Estimating Groundspeed and ETA
- ❑ VOR, GPS, or ADF Navigation (VR/IR), based on aircraft equipment
- ❑ Position Fix by Navigation Facilities
- ❑ Lost Procedures
- ❑ Diversion
- ❑ Autopilot Use, if equipped

BASIC INSTRUMENT MANEUVERS
Control and maneuvering solely by reference to instruments
- ❑ Straight-and-Level Flight (IR)
- ❑ Constant Airspeed Climbs (IR)
- ❑ Constant Airspeed Descents (IR)
- ❑ Turns to Headings (IR)
- ❑ Recovery from Unusual Flight Attitudes (IR)
- ❑ Using Radio Communications, Navigation Systems/Facilities, and ATC Services (IR)

STAGE III ■ Flight Training Syllabus

STAGE III ■ **Flight Training Syllabus**

EMERGENCY OPERATIONS
❑ Systems and Equipment Malfunctions
❑ Emergency Descent
❑ Emergency Approach and Landing (Simulated)
❑ Emergency Equipment and Survival Gear

TAKEOFFS, LANDINGS, AND GO-AROUNDS
❑ Takeoff Briefing
❑ Before Landing Briefing
❑ Rejected Takeoff
❑ Go-Around/Rejected Landing
❑ Forward Slip to a Landing
❑ Normal and Crosswind Takeoffs and Landings
❑ Short- and Soft-Field Takeoffs and Landings

POSTFLIGHT PROCEDURES
❑ After Landing, Parking, and Securing

COMPLETION STANDARDS
- Demonstrate satisfactory knowledge, risk management, and skills associated with all maneuvers and procedures required by the Private Pilot Airman Certification Standards.
- Demonstrate proficiency in performing each assigned maneuver according to the criteria established by the Private Pilot Airman Certification Standards.
- Demonstrate single-pilot resource management (SRM) skills, including aeronautical decision-making (ADM), and risk management.
- Demonstrate mastery of the airplane so that the successful outcome of each task performed is never in doubt.
- Demonstrate sound understanding of the knowledge, skill, and proficiency requirements for private pilot certification.

POSTFLIGHT DEBRIEFING
❑ Evaluate maneuvers/procedures and SRM.
❑ Plan additional instruction for skills that do not meet course completion standards.
❑ Update the record folder and logbook.

Appendix A — Pilot Briefing Questions

This appendix provides you with the necessary material to complete the Presolo Exam and the pilot briefing sessions, which are assigned in the syllabus. Each briefing is a series of questions designed to provide a systematic method of checking the student's knowledge level.

Each briefing should be completed before the appropriate flight lesson to gain optimum benefit. The student should demonstrate understanding of the questions and any additional questions that develop during the briefing.

PRESOLO EXAM BRIEFING

FAR 61.87 outlines the requirements for student pilot solo flights. As specified in this regulation, the student must demonstrate satisfactory knowledge of the required subject areas by completing a knowledge test.

This exam is to be administered and graded by the instructor who endorses the student pilot certificate for solo flight. Flight instructors must include questions on applicable portions of FAR Parts 61 and 91. In addition, instructors should modify the exam as necessary to make it appropriate for the aircraft to be flown and the local flying environment.

Students should complete the Presolo Exam using the booklet in their private pilot training kit. The questions are included here for instructor use.

GENERAL QUESTIONS

1. What personal documents and endorsements are you required to have before you fly solo? [FAR 61.87]
2. What are your student pilot limitations regarding carriage of passengers or cargo and flying for compensation or hire? [FAR 61.89]
3. Explain student pilot limitations concerning visibility and flight above clouds. [FAR 61.89]
4. Who has the final authority and responsibility for the operation of the airplane when you are flying solo? [FAR 1.1, 91.3, 91.7]
5. Discuss what preflight action concerning the airport and aircraft performance is specified in the regulations for a local flight. [FAR 91.103]
6. During engine runup, you cause rocks, debris, and propeller blast to be directed toward another aircraft or person. Could this be considered careless or reckless operations of an aircraft? [FAR 91.13]
7. You may not fly as pilot of a civil aircraft within _____ hours after consumption of any alcoholic beverage, or while having _____ % or greater of alcohol in your blood. [91.17]

8. What are the general requirements pertaining to the use of safety belts and shoulder harnesses? [FAR 91.105, 91.107]

9. What is the minimum fuel reserve for day VFR flight, and on what cruise speed is the fuel reserve based? [FAR 91.151]

10. A transponder with Mode C is required at all times in all airspace at and above _____ feet MSL, except below _____ feet AGL. [FAR 91.215]

11. What aircraft certificates and documents must be on board when you are flying solo? [FAR 91.203, 91.9, 23.1519]

12. No person may operate an aircraft so close to another aircraft as to create a _____. [FAR 91.111]

13. Who has the right-of-way when two aircraft are on final approach to land at the same time? [FAR 91.113]

14. What action do you need to take if you are overtaking another aircraft and which aircraft has the right-of-way? What should you do if you are flying a head-on collision course with another aircraft? If another airplane is converging from the right, who has the right-of-way? [FAR 91.113]

15. Except when necessary for takeoffs and landings, what are the minimum safe altitudes when flying over congested and uncongested areas? [FAR 91.119]

16. If an altimeter setting is not available at an airport, what setting should you use before departing on a local flight? [FAR 91.121]

17. What altitudes should you use when operating under VFR in level cruising flight at more than 3,000 feet AGL? [FAR 91.159]

18. When practicing steep turns, stalls, and maneuvering during slow flight, the entry altitude must allow a recovery to be completed no lower than _____ feet AGL.

19. When is a go-around appropriate?

20. What general steps should you follow after an engine failure in flight?

AIRPLANE QUESTIONS

If necessary, the instructor may include additional questions pertaining to the make and model of airplane to be flown.

1. List the minimum equipment and instruments that must be working properly in your airplane for day VFR flight. [FAR 91.205]

APPENDIX A ■ Pilot Briefing Questions

Private Pilot Syllabus

2. Fill in the V-speed definitions and the corresponding speed for your airplane.

	Definition	Speed
V_{S0}	_____	_____
V_{S1}	_____	_____
V_X	_____	_____
V_Y	_____	_____
V_{FE}	_____	_____
V_A	_____	_____
V_{NO}	_____	_____
V_{NE}	_____	_____

3. What is the best glide speed for your training airplane?
4. What is the maximum allowable flap setting for takeoff in your airplane?
5. The total usable fuel capacity for your airplane is _____ gallons. On a standard day (sea level, temperature: 15°C, altimeter: 29.92 inches Hg), the fuel consumption rate during normal (approximately 75% power) cruise is _____ gallons per hour.
6. What grades of fuel can be safely used in your airplane? What are the colors of the recommended fuels? What happens to the color of the fuel if two grades are mixed?
7. The maximum oil capacity of your airplane is _____ quarts, and the minimum oil capacity to begin a flight is _____ quarts.
8. The maximum crosswind component specified by your instructor for solo takeoffs and landings in the training airplane is _____ knots. [FAR 61.89]
9. When do you use carburetor heat? What are the indications of carburetor icing?
10. What is the takeoff and landing distance over a 50-foot obstacle for your airplane at your airport? Assume maximum certificated takeoff weight, 80°F, winds calm, and an altimeter setting of 29.52.

AIRPORT AND LOCAL AIRSPACE QUESTIONS

Flight instructors may assign only those questions that pertain to the student's airport environment and surrounding local area. However, if necessary, instructors may assign additional questions for a particular flying area.

1. What are the traffic patterns for each runway at your airport? What is the MSL altitude for the traffic pattern?
2. How do you enter and exit the traffic pattern at your airport? What, if any, radio communications are required? [AIM] [AC 90-66]
3. What radio calls are recommended in the traffic pattern at an uncontrolled airport? What radio calls are required at your airport? [AIM]

APPENDIX A ■ Pilot Briefing Questions

4. What is the standard direction of turns in the traffic pattern? Give an example of a visual display indicating a nonstandard traffic pattern. [AIM]

5. What is CTAF? Explain CTAF procedures at your training airport(s). [AIM]

6. How can you determine if a runway is closed? [AIM]

7. What are the typical dimensions of Class D airspace and what requirement(s) must be met prior to entry? [FAR 91.129]

8. What is the maximum speed permitted for aircraft below 10,000 feet MSL? What is the maximum speed allowed in Class B airspace? What is the maximum speed allowed in a VFR corridor through Class B airspace? [FAR 91.117]

9. If you receive ATC instructions that you feel may compromise safety or will cause you to violate an FAR, what should you do? [FAR 91.123]

10. What is the meaning of each of the following ATC light signals on the ground and in flight? [FAR 91.125]
    ◊ Steady green
    ◊ Flashing green
    ◊ Steady red
    ◊ Flashing red
    ◊ Flashing white
    ◊ Alternating red and green

11. In addition to equipment requirements and a student pilot certificate, what other requirement(s), if any, must be met before a student pilot is authorized to fly solo within Class B airspace? [FAR 61.95]

12. Explain the general transponder equipment and use requirement(s) when operating within or near Class B airspace. [FAR 91.215]

13. Describe the Class B airspace boundaries that affect your airport, or an airport nearby. Explain how you can use navigation equipment and ground reference points to identify the Class B boundaries. (Draw a diagram, if necessary.)

14. You have called ATC just prior to entering the Class B airspace, and the controller tells you to, "Squawk 2466 and ident." Are you now allowed to enter the Class B airspace without any further instructions? Explain. [FAR 91.131]

15. On a sectional chart, what does a dashed magenta line around the airport indicate?

16. Explain the minimum visibility and ceiling requirements for VFR flight in Class D airspace.

17. May a student pilot request a special VFR clearance in Class D airspace when visibility is less than three miles? Explain your answer. [FAR 61.89, 91.157]

18. You have called ATC prior to entering Class C airspace, and the controller responds with your call sign and tells you to "Standby." Are you now allowed to enter this airspace without any further instructions? [AIM]

19. Describe the typical dimensions of Class C airspace. Is participation in the radar service mandatory within the outer area of Class C airspace?

20. Describe the Class C boundaries that affect your airport, or an airport nearby. Explain how you can use navigation equipment and ground reference points to identify the Class C inner and outer circles, as well as the outer area. (Draw a diagram, if necessary.)

SOLO CROSS-COUNTRY BRIEFING

Although the student has flown solo before the solo cross-country, regulations require that the student receive additional ground and flight instruction prior to conducting solo cross-country flight. The following briefing is designed to assist the instructor in determining if the student has an acceptable level of knowledge to conduct these operations safely.

1. Plan a cross-country flight by obtaining a weather briefing and completing a navigation log.
2. Select at least 10 examples of good checkpoints along your route of flight. Also, select at least 10 checkpoints that would be difficult to see from the air.
3. By referring to the chart used to plan the cross-country, determine all you can about the destination airport.
4. Where can you find additional information about the destination airport?
5. Can you buy fuel at your destination?
6. Explain how to determine your position by using VOR, ADF, or GPS, and how you can use these navigation systems to fly to your destination.
7. Once airborne, how will you open your flight plan?
8. If you determine you are falling behind your ETA, what action should you take?
9. Upon arrival at your destination, how will you close your flight plan? [AIM]
10. If your flight plan is not closed, how long after your ETA will a search begin?
11. If you have a problem with the airplane enroute, where can you land?
12. Explain how to obtain current weather reports and forecasts while enroute. What will you do if the weather along your route of flight deteriorates? [AIM]
13. If you become lost, what will you do?
14. What are the minimum VFR fuel reserves required by FARs for day and night flight? [FAR 91.151]

APPENDIX A ■ Pilot Briefing Questions

PRIVATE PILOT PRACTICAL TEST BRIEFING

This is the last pilot briefing and one of the most important, because it prepares the student for the practical test. Remember that there is not any formal division between the oral and flight portions of the practical test. Oral questioning can be used at any time to determine whether the student's knowledge of a subject area is adequate.

The briefing should be conducted on a private, individual basis in a manner similar to an actual practical test. The following sample questions indicate the types of questions an examiner might ask a candidate. Practical test preparation should include a discussion of FAR Parts 61, 91, and NTSB 830, emphasizing the rules that apply to private pilots. You can also anticipate that the examiner will ask specific questions about the required flight maneuvers, as well as the airplane and its systems. A useful aid when preparing for oral questioning is the student's airman knowledge test results. Discuss each incorrectly-answered FAA question subject, because the examiner is likely to emphasize these areas.

AIRCRAFT CERTIFICATES AND DOCUMENTS

1. What documents must be on board the aircraft before operation? Where are they normally located?
2. Who is responsible for determining whether an aircraft is safe for flight?
3. Must the engine and aircraft logbooks be carried on board the aircraft? [91.417]
4. Locate the last annual inspection in the aircraft logbooks and determine when the next inspection is due. [FAR 91.409]
5. If the engine logbook does not reflect a current annual inspection but the aircraft logbook does, is the aircraft legal for operation?
6. When is a 100-hour inspection required?
7. If the aircraft has a transponder, locate its last inspection in the logbook. When is its next inspection due? [FAR 91.413]
8. If an airplane is equipped with a transponder and the aircraft logbook indicates the inspection has expired, can the transponder still be used? [FAR 91.413]
9. Describe the items that you can use to determine the operating limitations of the aircraft. [FAR 91.9]
10. Where can you find the aircraft's empty weight and moment? What is the empty weight and moment for your airplane?

AIRPLANE SYSTEMS

1. What is the minimum grade of fuel required for operation of your airplane? What color is the fuel?

2. If the specified grade of fuel is not available, should you use a lower or higher than normal grade? Why?

3. What is the total fuel capacity of the aircraft? How much fuel is unusable?

4. Where is the fuel selector located? What is the correct procedure for switching fuel tanks, if appropriate?

5. What is the purpose of an auxiliary electric fuel pump? When should you use it?

6. What is the purpose of the fuel tank quick drains?

7. What is the purpose of the fuel tank vent?

8. When should you check the fuel tanks for fuel contamination?

9. What are some ways to reduce the possibility of fuel contamination?

10. What is the electrical system voltage when the alternator is running? What is the battery voltage?

11. Does your airplane have a generator or an alternator? Does it produce alternating current (AC) or direct current (DC)?

12. What are the basic advantages of an alternator over a generator?

13. What is the purpose of the voltage regulator?

14. How do you detect alternator or generator failure?

15. Why is an ammeter or load meter installed in the airplane, and what does each indicate?

16. Is the electrical system protected by circuit breakers or fuses?

17. What is the procedure for resetting a tripped circuit breaker?

18. Describe how you should use the primer during cold and warm weather operations.

19. After priming the engine during a cold weather start, is it advisable to "pump" the throttle after engaging the starter? Explain.

20. During a cold weather start, the oil pressure gauge does not indicate any oil pressure for nearly 30 seconds. What should you do?

21. During the magneto check before takeoff, when you switch from BOTH to the RIGHT position, the rpm remains the same as it was in the BOTH position. Does this mean that the aircraft has an exceptionally good magneto? Explain.

22. Is it possible for carburetor icing to develop during a taxi operation? Explain.

23. Should you normally use carburetor heat during the takeoff? Explain.

24. What might cause engine roughness during runup at a high elevation field (5,000 feet MSL) during hot weather? What action is appropriate in this situation?

25. What is the first indication of carburetor icing on an airplane with a fixed-pitch or a constant-speed propeller?

APPENDIX A ■ **Pilot Briefing Questions**

26. What methods should you use to decrease or prevent engine overheating during climbs?

27. Describe the technique to achieve a lean fuel mixture during cruise flight.

28. Define the term "basic empty weight."

29. Is it acceptable to use the empty weight posted in the pilot's operating handbook sample problem for weight and balance computations? Explain.

30. What is the "reference datum?" Where is it located on this aircraft?

31. Define the term "allowable center of gravity (or moment) range." [FAA-H-8083-1 Aircraft Weight and Balance Handbook]

32. What is the center of gravity (or moment) range for your training airplane at its maximum takeoff weight?

33. Compute a weight and balance problem for the actual flight test conditions. Does the center of gravity (or moment) fall within limits?

34. What flight characteristics may you expect if the aircraft is loaded with the CG too far forward or too far aft?

35. What is the maximum allowable baggage weight if the CG is within the center of gravity envelope?

36. How do you know if the weight and balance data of the airplane have been changed? How is the change and the nature of the modification recorded?

PERFORMANCE

1. Indicate 5 to 10 factors that can affect takeoff distance.

2. Compute the density altitude given the following conditions:
   ◊ Field elevation: 5,000 ft
   ◊ Altimeter: 30.12 inches Hg
   ◊ Outside air temperature: 35°C

Use the airplane flight manual/pilot's operating handbook of the airplane that you will use for the practical test to answer questions 3 through 9.

3. Given the following conditions, compute the takeoff distance.
   ◊ Airplane configuration: as specified on performance chart
   ◊ Runway: hard surfaced
   ◊ Aircraft weight: maximum takeoff
   ◊ Headwind: 10 knots
   ◊ Field elevation: 4,000 ft
   ◊ Outside air temperature: 29°C

4. Given the following conditions, determine the landing distance.
   ◊ Airplane configuration: as specified on performance chart
   ◊ Runway: hard surfaced
   ◊ Aircraft weight: maximum landing
   ◊ Headwind: 10 knots
   ◊ Field elevation: 3,000 ft
   ◊ Outside air temperature: 10°C

5. Calculate the time, fuel, and distance you will need to complete a climb from sea level to 8,500 feet.

6. During a short-field landing, what technique provides maximum braking effectiveness?

7. When landing on a sod runway, should you expect a longer or a shorter than normal landing roll? What should you expect on a runway covered with water, snow, or slush?

8. Define best angle-of-climb and best rate-of-climb airspeed. What are these air- speeds for your airplane?

9. How do you convert indicated to calibrated airspeed? Is this conversion necessary during normal operations?

LIMITATIONS

1. Under which category is your airplane certificated? Are spins approved?

2. What is the maximum positive G-loading approved in this airplane with the flaps up? What is the maximum G-loading with flaps down?

3. State the V-speed value of each color code on the airspeed indicator and define its meaning and significance.

	Speed	Definition
◊ White	_____	_____
◊ Green	_____	_____
◊ Yellow	_____	_____
◊ Red	_____	_____

4. Define maneuvering speed and its significance to the airplane. Is this speed designated by a colored marking on the airspeed indicator?

5. What other airspeed limitations exist for this airplane?

6. What are the maximum takeoff and landing weights for this airplane?

WEATHER AND CROSS-COUNTRY FLIGHT PLANNING

1. How can you obtain weather reports and forecasts? Where do you find a listing of appropriate telephone numbers?

2. How can you update weather reports and forecasts during flight?

3. If your destination does not issue a terminal aerodrome forecast, how can you determine the forecast weather at your ETA?

4. What is a PIREP? How significant is it? [AIM, AC 00-45]

5. Plan a cross-country flight, obtain a complete weather briefing, and complete a navigation log.

6. Is the weather satisfactory for the planned flight? If not, could a change in routing or a delay in the planned departure time allow you to proceed with the flight?

7. If weather deteriorates enroute, what should you do?

8. If you encounter moderate to severe turbulence, is it advisable to slow the airplane below what speed? Explain.

9. If you discover you are lost, what should you do?

APPENDIX A ■ Pilot Briefing Questions

AERONAUTICAL CHARTS
AND AIRPORT OPERATIONS

To answer questions 1 through 20, the student should use a sectional chart appropriate to the local area. Select a controlled airport and an uncontrolled airport to answer the first 10 questions.

1. Provide at least 10 different items of information pertaining to the controlled airport.

2. Is Class D airspace designated around the controlled airport? If so, when is it in effect?

3. What is the minimum MSL altitude you can use to overfly a tower-controlled airport without establishing two-way communications with the control tower? [FAR 91.129, 91.159]

4. At what times is the control tower in operation at this airport?

5. If you cannot contact the control tower on the normal frequency, can you receive an airport advisory on the UNICOM frequency? Explain. [AIM]

6. What frequency should you use to obtain an airport advisory at the uncontrolled airport? [AIM]

7. What frequencies can you use to communicate Flight Service in the area?

8. What is the minimum weather required at the uncontrolled airport before you can land under VFR? [FAR 91.155, 91.157]

9. Is it legal to enter Class D airspace without establishing two-way radio communications? [FAR 91.155]

10. At an uncontrolled airport, what is the proper procedure for determining the runway in use? How do you enter the traffic pattern? [FAR 91.127, AIM]

11. How are VORs, VORTACs, and VOR/DMEs identified on a sectional chart?

12. Are VOR radials aligned to magnetic or true north?

13. Locate an example of each of the following types of airspace and explain its lateral and vertical limits, as well as its significance to a VFR flight.
    ◊ Class D
    ◊ Class E
    ◊ Uncontrolled airspace (Class G)
    ◊ Restricted airspace
    ◊ Military operations area (MOA)
    ◊ Military training route (MTR)

14. Locate an MTR on the sectional chart. Explain all you can about the MTR, based on its designation.

15. Where can you obtain current temporary flight restrictions (TFRs)?

16. Obtain a current TFR and draw the airspace limits on the appropriate sectional or terminal chart.

17. What is the Washington DC Special Flight Rules Area? What is the flight restricted zone (FRZ)?

18. What is an air defense identification zone (ADIZ)?

19. On the sectional chart, locate an airport within Class D airspace. If the weather at that airport is reported as IFR due to ground fog, would you need to establish two-way communications with the control tower to fly VFR through the lateral limits of this Class D airspace area at 6,000 feet AGL? [FAR 91.129, 91.155]

20. Assuming the airport is reporting a 600-foot ceiling and one-mile visibility, could you conduct a VFR flight to and from the airport? [FAR 61.89, 91.155, 91.157]

21. What are the VFR and special VFR weather minimums for Class D airspace? [FAR 91.155, 91.157]

22. Locate an obstruction on the sectional chart. Immediately adjacent to it are two numbers (one in parentheses). What is the significance of each number?

23. If the DME is tuned to a VOR facility, what indications can you expect from the DME?

24. Locate a maximum elevation figure (MEF). Explain its significance.

25. Explain proper control wheel positioning for crosswind taxiing.

26. Relative to directional control, what must you be aware of during takeoff in a strong crosswind?

27. Describe the symbols on an airport that indicate either left-hand or right-hand traffic patterns.

28. Discuss the different colors associated with airport lighting and what each represents.

COLLISION AVOIDANCE

1. Which aircraft has the right-of-way over all other aircraft? [FAR 91.113]

2. Two aircraft of the same category are converging at the same approximate altitude. Which aircraft has the right-of-way? [FAR 91.113]

3. If a glider and an airplane are approaching head-on, or nearly so, who has the right-of-way and what action should be taken? [FAR 91.113]

4. One aircraft is on final approach and the second is waiting to take off. Which aircraft has the right-of-way? [FAR 91.113]

POSTFLIGHT PROCEDURES

1. After landing, what procedures should you follow concerning the shutdown, parking, and securing of your airplane?

2. After shutdown, why is it important to make sure the ignition switch has been placed in the OFF position?

3. When should you refuel the airplane? What are some precautionary steps that you should take during refueling?

APPENDIX A ■ Pilot Briefing Questions

NIGHT OPERATIONS

1. What are the differences between scanning for aircraft at night and during the day? [AIM]
2. Why is it important to carry a flashlight at night?
3. Is it easier or more difficult to avoid obstructions at night? Explain.
4. Is weather easier or more difficult to avoid at night? Explain.
5. How is a night takeoff different from one performed during the day? Explain.
6. Is a night approach flown differently than one flown during the day? Explain any differences.

EMERGENCY OPERATIONS

1. What is the definition of the best or maximum glide speed? What is the best glide speed for your airplane?
2. What is the approximate glide ratio for your airplane.
3. Discuss the procedures to be used if a partial or complete engine failure occurs.
4. If an engine fire develops during flight, what steps should you follow?
5. What procedure should you use if an electrical fire occurs?
6. While in flight, you note that the oil pressure is low, but the oil temperature remains normal. Explain what action you would take in this situation.
7. During flight, the engine oil pressure suddenly drops to zero and the oil temperature begins to rise. Explain what has happened and what action you would take in this situation.
8. After takeoff, your engine suddenly stops at an altitude of 100 feet AGL. What action should you take?

AERODYNAMICS

1. Discuss the aerodynamic factors associated with stalls and spins.
2. At what indicated airspeed will your airplane stall at maximum takeoff weight with flaps down and power off?
3. What increase in stall speed can you expect in a 60° bank in the clean configuration?
4. What is an accelerated stall, and when is it most likely to occur? What are the typical causes of a spin, and how do you recover?
5. If you are operating the airplane at a low airspeed with full power during a descent, what action should you take to arrest the descent? Why?
6. Explain ground effect and how you can take advantage of it during takeoff.

REGULATIONS AND THE AERONAUTICAL INFORMATION MANUAL

1. How wide is a Victor airway? [FAR 71.75]

2. What is the significance of 14,500 feet MSL in the classification of airspace?

3. What type of information is in the Aeronautical Information Manual?

4. At what time of day may you begin logging night flight time? [FAR 1.1, 61.51, 61.57]

5. At what time must you turn on the aircraft position lights? [FAR 91.209]

6. What are the recency of experience requirements to carry passengers at night in a particular category and class of aircraft? [FAR 61.57]

7. Must an airplane always be equipped with an emergency locator transmitter? If not, explain the exceptions. [FAR 91.207]

8. When must your passengers be supplied supplemental oxygen? When are you, as pilot in command, required to use oxygen? [FAR 91.211]

9. When are passengers required to wear safety belts and, if installed, shoulder harnesses? [FAR 91.107]

10. What is the minimum allowable flight altitude over a sparsely populated area? [FAR 91.119]

11. Under what circumstances is it legal to drop an object from an aircraft while in flight? [FAR 91.15]

12. Are flight plans required for VFR cross-country flight?

13. What are the pilot and equipment requirements for operation within Class B airspace? [FAR 91.131(b), 61.95].

14. What are the pilot and equipment requirements for operation within Class C airspace? [FAR 91.130]

15. Who may give a flight review? How often must you obtain one? [FAR 61.56]

16. For a private pilot, what are the restrictions to acting as pilot in command of an airplane with more than 200 horsepower? What about an airplane with retractable landing gear, flaps, and a controllable-pitch propeller? [FAR 61.31]

17. According to NTSB 830, what is an aircraft accident and when must it be reported? What is the difference between an accident and an incident? [NTSB 830.5]

APPENDIX A ■ Pilot Briefing Questions

INTERCEPTION

1. What are the three intercept phases? [AIM]

2. What steps must you immediately take upon interception? [AIM]

3. If you are intercepted and unable to establish radio communication, how can you advise the intercepting aircraft you are in distress? [AIM]

AEROMEDICAL FACTORS

1. Discuss the similarities and differences between hypoxia, hyperventilation, and carbon monoxide poisoning. What are the symptoms and effects for each condition and what corrective actions should you take in each case?

2. If a passenger exhibits symptoms that could be attributed to more than one condition, what should you do? [AIM]

3. What are the rules concerning the use of alcohol and the operation of an aircraft? [FAR 91.17]

4. Name several common medications that you should not take before or during a flight.

5. What is spatial disorientation, when is it most likely to occur, and what corrective action should you take if you become spatially disoriented?

6. What are the effects of fatigue on a pilot?

Appendix B — FAR Requirements

PRIVATE PILOT FLIGHT TRAINING

FAR 61.87 — SOLO REQUIREMENTS FOR STUDENT PILOTS

This table specifies the flight lessons in which each task required by FAR 61.87 is introduced, reviewed, and evaluated. The name of the task as it appears in the syllabus lessons is shown in bold if it differs from the task name as shown in FAR 61.87. Use the check boxes to ensure each required task is completed before the student receives an instructor endorsement for solo flight.

FL means Flight Lesson with additional distinctions for solo (S), night (N) and cross-country (C) flights. (Example: FL 21SC is Flight Lesson 21 Solo Cross-Country)

APPENDIX B ■ FAR Requirements

PART 61 SUBPART C — STUDENT PILOTS
FAR 61.87 SOLO REQUIREMENTS FOR STUDENT PILOTS
(D) MANEUVERS AND PROCEDURES FOR PRE-SOLO FLIGHT TRAINING IN A SINGLE-ENGINE AIRPLANE.

	TASKS	STAGE	INTRODUCE	REVIEW	EVALUATE
1. ☐	Preflight planning and preparation **Preflight Preparation**	I	FL1	FL 2, 3, 4	FL 10
		II	FL 16N, 17C	FL 18NC, 19SC	FL 20
		III	NA	FL 21S, 22S, 23, 24	FL 25, 26
1. ☐	Powerplant operation and operation of systems **Operation of Systems**	I	FL 1	FL 2	FL 10
		II	FL 16N, 17C	FL 18NC, 19SC	FL 20
		III	NA	FL 21SC, 22SC, 23, 24S	25, 26
2. ☐	Taxiing or surface operations, including runups **Taxiing**	I	FL 1	FL 2, 7, 8, 9S	FL 10
		II	FL 16N	FL 12S	NA
		III	NA	FL 23, 24	FL 25, 26
2. ☐	Taxiing or surface operations, including runups **Before Takeoff Check/Runup**	I	FL 1	FL 2, 9S	FL 10
		II	FL 16N	FL 12S	NA
		III	NA	FL 23, 24	FL 25, 26
3. ☐	Takeoffs and landings, including normal and crosswind **Normal Takeoff and Climb** **Normal Approach and Landing**	I	FL 1	FL 2, 3, 4, 5, 7, 8, 9S	FL 10
		II	FL 16N	FL 12S, 13S, 15, 16N	FL 20
		III	NA	FL 23, 24,	FL 25, 26

Table continued on next page.

APPENDIX B ■ FAR Requirements

	TASKS	STAGE	INTRODUCE	REVIEW	EVALUATE
3. ☐	Takeoffs and landings, including normal and crosswind	I	FL 6	FL 7, 8	FL 10
	Crosswind Takeoff and Climb	II	FL 16N	FL 13S, 15, 16N	FL 20
	Crosswind Approach and Landing	III	NA	FL 23, 24	FL 25, 26
4. ☐	Straight-and-level flight, and turns in both directions	I	FL 1	FL 2	NA
		II	NA	NA	NA
	Straight-and-Level Flight	III	NA	NA	NA
4. ☐	Straight-and-level flight, and turns in both directions	I	FL1	FL 2, 3	NA
	Turns in Both Directions	II	NA	NA	NA
		III	NA	NA	NA
5. ☐	Climbs and climbing turns	I	FL 1, 2	FL 2, 3	NA
	Climbs and Descents	II	NA	NA	NA
	Climbs and Climbing Turns	III	NA	NA	NA
6. ☐	Airport traffic patterns, including entry and departure procedures	I	FL 2	FL 3, 7, 8, 9S	FL 10
	Traffic Patterns/Departure, Arrival, Entry, and Approach Procedures	II	NA	FL 11, 12S 17C, 18NC, 19S	FL 20
		III	NA	FL 21S, 22S, 23, 24	FL 25, 26
7. ☐	Collision avoidance	I	FL 1	FL 2	NA
		II	FL 16N, 17C	18NC, 19S	FL 20
		III	NA	FL 21SC, 22SC	NA
7. ☐	Wind shear avoidance	I	FL 6	FL 7, 8	FL 10
		II	NA	FL 11, 17C, 18NC	FL 20
		III	NA	FL 23, 24	FL 25, 26
7. ☐	Wake turbulence avoidance	I	FL 6	FL 7, 8	FL 10
		II	NA	FL 11, 17C, 18NC	NA
		III	NA	FL 23, 24	FL 25, 26
8. ☐	Descents, with and without turns, using high and low drag configurations	I	FL 1	FL 2, 3	NA
	Climbs and Descents	II	NA	NA	NA
	Descents and Descending Turns in High and Low Drag Configurations	III	NA	NA	NA

Table continued on next page.

Private Pilot Syllabus

	TASKS	STAGE	INTRODUCE	REVIEW	EVALUATE
9. ☐	Flight at various airspeeds from cruise to slow flight	I	FL 2	FL 3	NA
		II	NA	NA	NA
		III	NA	NA	NA
10. ☐	Stall entries from various flight attitudes and power combinations with recovery initiated at the first indication of a stall, and recovery from a full stall	I	FL 3	FL 4, 5, 7	FL 10
		II	FL 16N	FL 13S	NA
		III	NA	FL 23, 24	FL 25, 26
11. ☐	Emergency procedures and equipment malfunctions **Emergency Operations**	I	FL 4	FL 5, 7, 8	FL 10
		II	NA	FL 17C, 18NC	FL 20
		III	NA	FL 23, 24	FL 25, 26
11. ☐	Emergency procedures and equipment malfunctions **Systems and Equipment Malfunctions**	I	FL 4	FL 5, 7, 8	FL 10
		II	NA	FL 17, 18NC	FL 20
		III	NA	FL 23, 24	FL 25, 26
12. ☐	Ground reference maneuvers	I	FL 5	FL 6, 7	FL 10
		II	NA	FL 13S	NA
		III	NA	FL 23, 24	FL 25, 26
13. ☐	Approaches to a landing area with simulated engine malfunctions **Emergency Approach and Landing (Simulated)**	I	FL 4	FL 5, 7	FL 10
		II	NA	FL 17C, 18NC	FL 20
		III	NA	FL 23, 24	FL 25, 26
14. ☐	Slips to a landing **Forward Slip to a Landing**	I	FL 6	FL 7, 8	FL 10
		II	NA	NA	NA
		III	NA	FL 23, 24	FL 25, 26
15. ☐	Go-arounds **Go-Around/Rejected Landing**	I	FL 6	FL 7, 8, 9S	FL 10
		II	FL 16N	NA	NA
		III	NA	FL 23, 24	FL 25, 26

APPENDIX B ■ FAR Requirements

PRIVATE PILOT FLIGHT TRAINING

FAR 61.93 — SOLO CROSS-COUNTRY FLIGHT REQUIREMENTS

This table specifies the flight lessons in which each task required by FAR 61.93 is introduced, reviewed, and evaluated. The name of the task as it appears in the syllabus lessons is shown in bold if it differs from the task name as shown in FAR 61.93. Use the check boxes to ensure each required task is completed before the student receives an instructor endorsement for solo cross-country flight.

FL means Flight Lesson with additional distinctions for solo (S), night (N) and cross-country (C) flights. (Example: FL 21SC is Flight Lesson 21 Solo Cross-Country)

PART 61 SUBPART C — STUDENT PILOTS
61.93 SOLO CROSS-COUNTRY FLIGHT REQUIREMENTS
(E) MANEUVERS AND PROCEDURES FOR CROSS-COUNTRY FLIGHT TRAINING IN A SINGLE-ENGINE AIRPLANE.

	TASKS	STAGE	INTRODUCE	REVIEW	EVALUATE
1.	Use of aeronautical charts for VFR navigation using pilotage and dead reckoning with the aid of a magnetic compass	I	NA	NA	NA
		II	FL 17C	FL 18NC, 19S,	FL 20
	PREFLIGHT PREPARATION **Aeronautical Charts** **Pilotage and Dead Reckoning** **Cross-Country Flight Planning** **NAVIGATION** **Pilotage** **Dead Reckoning** **Estimating Groundspeed and ETA**	III	NA	FL 21S, 22S, 23, 24	FL 25, 26
2.	Use of aircraft performance charts pertaining to cross-country flight	I	NA	NA	NA
	Performance and Limitations	II	FL 17C	FL 18NC, 19S,	FL 20,
		III	NA	FL 21SC, 22SC, 23, 24	FL 25, 26
3.	Procurement and analysis of aeronautical weather reports and forecasts, including recognition of critical weather situations and estimating visibility while in flight	I	FL 3	FL 4	FL 10
		II	FL 17C	FL 18NC, 19S,	FL 20
	Weather Information **Estimating Visibility in Flight**	III	NA	FL 21SC, 22SC, 23, 24	FL 25, 26
4.	Emergency procedures	I	FL 4	FL 5, 7, 8	FL 10
	Emergency Operations	II	NA	FL 17C, 18NC	FL 20
		III	NA	FL 23, 24	FL 25, 26
5.	Traffic pattern procedures that include area departure, area arrival, entry into the traffic pattern, and approach	I	FL 2	FL 3, 7, 8, 9S	FL 10
	Traffic Patterns/Departure, Arrival, Entry, and Approach Procedures	II	NA	FL 11, 12S 17C, 18NC, 19S	FL 20
		III	NA	FL 21S, 22S, 23, 24	FL 25, 26

Table continued on next page.

	Tasks	Stage	Introduce	Review	Evaluate
6.	Procedures and operating practices for collision avoidance, wake turbulence precautions, and wind shear avoidance	I	FL 1	FL 2	NA
		II	FL 16N, 17C	18NC, 19S	FL 20
		III	NA	FL 21SC, 22SC	NA
6.	Procedures and operating practices for collision avoidance, wake turbulence precautions, and wind shear avoidance	I	FL 6	FL 7, 8	FL 10
		II	NA	FL 11, 17C, 18NC	NA
		III	NA	FL 23, 24	FL 25, 26
7.	Recognition, avoidance, and operational restrictions of hazardous terrain features in the geographical area where the cross-country flight will be flown **CFIT Avoidance**	I	NA	NA	NA
		II	FL 17C	FL 18NC, 19SC,	FL 20
		III	NA	21SC, 22SC	NA
8.	Procedures for operating the instruments and equipment installed in the aircraft to be flown, including recognition and use of the proper operational procedures and indications **Operation of Systems**	I	FL 1	FL 2	FL 10
		II	FL 16N, 17C	FL 18NC, 19SC	FL 20
		III	NA	FL 21SC, 22SC, 23, 24S	25, 26
9.	Use of radios for VFR navigation and two-way communication **VOR Navigation GPS Navigation ADF Navigation VOR, GPS, or ADF Navigation, based on aircraft equipment Position Fix by Navigation Facilities**	I	NA	NA	NA
		II	FL 14, 17C, 18NC	FL 15, 19SC	FL 20
		III	NA	FL 21SC, 22SC, 23, 24	FL 25, 26
9.	Use of radios for VFR navigation and two-way communication **Radio Communications**	I	FL 2	FL 3, 7, 8, 9S	FL 10
		II	NA	FL 11, 12S, 13S, 17C, 18SC, 19SC	FL 20
		III	NA	FL 21S, 22S, 23, 24	FL 25, 26
10.	Takeoff, approach, and landing procedures, including short-field, soft-field, and crosswind takeoffs, approaches, and landings **Normal Takeoff and Climb Normal Approach and Landing**	I	FL 1	FL 2, 3, 4, 5, 7, 8, 9S	FL 10
		II	FL 16N	FL 12S, 13S, 15, 16N	FL 20
		III	NA	FL 23, 24,	FL 25, 26
10.	Takeoff, approach, and landing procedures, including short-field, soft-field, and crosswind takeoffs, approaches, and landings **Short-Field Takeoff and Maximum Performance Climb Short-Field Approach and Landing Soft-Field Takeoff and Climb Soft-Field Approach and Landing**	I	NA	NA	NA
		II	FL 11	FL 14, 15, 16	FL 20
		III	NA	FL 23, 24	FL 25, 26

Table continued on next page.

APPENDIX B ■ FAR Requirements

TASKS	STAGE	INTRODUCE	REVIEW	EVALUATE
10. Takeoff, approach, and landing procedures, including short-field, soft-field, and crosswind takeoffs, approaches, and landings	I	FL 6	FL 7, 8	FL 10
	II	FL 16N	FL 13S, 15, 16N	FL 20
☐ **Crosswind Takeoff and Climb** **Crosswind Approach and Landing** **Normal and Crosswind Takeoffs and Landings**	III	NA	FL 23, 24	FL 25, 26
11. Climbs at best angle and best rate	I	NA	NA	NA
☐	II	FL 11	FL 14	NA
	III	NA	NA	NA
12. Control and maneuvering solely by reference to flight instruments, including straight and level flight, turns, descents, climbs, and use of radio aids, and ATC directives	I	FL 3	FL 4, 5, 7	FL 23, 24
	II	NA	NA	NA
☐ **Straight-and-Level Flight** **Turns to Headings (IR)** **Climbing and Descending Turns (IR)** **Constant Airspeed Descents (IR)** **Constant Airspeed Climbs (IR)**	III	NA	FL 23, 24	FL 25, 26
12. Control and maneuvering solely by reference to flight instruments, including straight and level flight, turns, descents, climbs, and use of radio aids, and ATC directives	I	NA	NA	NA
	II	FL 14	FL 15, 17C, 18NC	FL 20
☐ **Using Radio Communications, Navigation Systems/Facilities, and ATC Services**	III	NA	FL 23, 24	FL 25, 26

PRIVATE PILOT GROUND TRAINING

PART 141 APPENDIX B — PRIVATE PILOT CERTIFICATION COURSE: AERONAUTICAL KNOWLEDGE

FAR 61.105 — AERONAUTICAL KNOWLEDGE

This table specifies the ground lessons in which each task required by Part 141 and Part 61 is presented in the Ground Training Syllabus. Use the check boxes to ensure each required aeronautical knowledge area is completed before the student receives credit for Part 141 ground training completion or an instructor endorsement to take the FAA Private Pilot Airmen Knowledge Test.

GL means Ground Lesson.

APPENDIX B TO PART 141 — PRIVATE PILOT CERTIFICATION COURSE

3. AERONAUTICAL KNOWLEDGE TRAINING

(B) GROUND TRAINING MUST INCLUDE THE FOLLOWING AERONAUTICAL KNOWLEDGE AREAS.

PART 61 SUBPART E — PRIVATE PILOTS

61.105 AERONAUTICAL KNOWLEDGE

(B) AERONAUTICAL KNOWLEDGE AREAS.

	AERONAUTICAL KNOWLEDGE	GROUND LESSON
1. ☐	Applicable Federal Aviation Regulations for private pilot privileges, limitations, and flight operations	GL 1, 2, 8, 12, 14
2. ☐	Accident reporting requirements of the National Transportation Safety Board	GL 8
3. ☐	Applicable subjects of the Aeronautical Information Manual and the appropriate FAA advisory circulars	GL 4, 5, 12, 13, 14
4. ☐	Aeronautical charts for VFR navigation using pilotage, dead reckoning, and navigation systems	GL 4
5. ☐	Radio communication procedures	GL 5
6. ☐	Recognition of critical weather situations from the ground and in flight, wind shear avoidance, and the procurement and use of aeronautical weather reports and forecasts	GL 7, 9
7. ☐	Safe and efficient operation of aircraft, including collision avoidance, and recognition and avoidance of wake turbulence	GL 4, 7
8. ☐	Effects of density altitude on takeoff and climb performance	GL 11
9. ☐	Weight and balance computations	GL 11
10. ☐	Principles of aerodynamics, powerplants, and aircraft systems	GL 2, 3
11. ☐	Stall awareness, spin entry, spins, and spin recovery techniques	GL 3
12. ☐	Aeronautical decision making and judgment	GL 1, 13
13. ☐	Preflight actions that include (1) how to obtain information on runway lengths at airports of intended use, data on takeoff and landing distances, weather reports and forecasts, and fuel requirements; and (2) how to plan for alternatives if the planned flight cannot be completed or delays are encountered	GL 5, 9, 11, 12, 14

PRIVATE PILOT FLIGHT TRAINING

PRIVATE PILOT — AIRPLANE AIRMAN CERTIFICATION STANDARDS

PART 141 APPENDIX B — PRIVATE PILOT CERTIFICATION COURSE: FLIGHT TRAINING

FAR 61.107 — FLIGHT PROFICIENCY

This table specifies the flight lessons in which each task required by Part 141, Part 61, and the Airman Certification Standards (ACS) is introduced, reviewed, and evaluated. The name of the task as it appears in the syllabus lessons is shown in bold if it differs from the task name as shown in the applicable FAR. Use the check boxes to ensure each required task is completed before the student receives credit for Part 141 flight training completion or an instructor endorsement to take the private pilot practical test.

FL means Flight Lesson with additional distinctions for solo (S), night (N) and cross-country (C) flights. (Example: FL 21SC is Flight Lesson 21 Solo Cross-Country)

APPENDIX B TO PART 141 — PRIVATE PILOT CERTIFICATION COURSE
4. FLIGHT TRAINING
(D) EACH APPROVED COURSE MUST INCLUDE THE FLIGHT TRAINING ON THE APPROVED AREAS OF OPERATION LISTED IN THIS PARAGRAPH THAT ARE APPROPRIATE TO THE AIRCRAFT CATEGORY AND CLASS RATING AREAS OF OPERATION
(1) FOR A SINGLE-ENGINE AIRPLANE COURSE

PART 61 SUBPART E — PRIVATE PILOTS
61.107 FLIGHT PROFICIENCY
(B) AREAS OF OPERATION
(1) FOR AN AIRPLANE CATEGORY RATING WITH A SINGLE-ENGINE CLASS RATING

PRIVATE PILOT — AIRPLANE AIRMAN CERTIFICATION STANDARDS

FAR/ACS	TASKS	STAGE	INTRODUCE	REVIEW	EVALUATE
Part 141 Appendix B (I) FAR 61.107 (I) ACS I.	Preflight Preparation				
ACS I. A. ☐	Pilot Qualifications	I	FL 1	FL 2	FL 10
		II	NA	NA	NA
		III	NA	FL 23, 24	FL 25, 26
ACS I. B. ☐	Airworthiness Requirements	I	FL 1	FL 2	FL 10
		II	FL 16N	NA	NA
		III	NA	FL 23, 24	FL 25, 26
ACS I. C. ☐	Weather Information	I	FL 3	FL 4	FL 10
		II	FL 17C, 18NC, 19SC	NA	FL 20
		III	NA	FL 21S, 22, 23, 24	FL 25, 26

Table continued on next page.

APPENDIX B ■ FAR Requirements

Private Pilot Syllabus

FAR/ACS	TASKS	STAGE	INTRODUCE	REVIEW	EVALUATE
ACS I. D. ☐	Cross-Country Flight Planning	I	NA	NA	NA
		II	FL 17C	FL 18N, 19S	FL 20
		III	NA	FL 21SC, 22SC, 23, 24	FL 25, 26
ACS I. E. ☐	National Airspace System	I	NA	NA	NA
		II	FL 17C	FL 18NC, 19SC	FL 20
		III	NA	FL 21SC, 22SC, 23, 24	FL 25, 26
ACS I. F. ☐	Performance and Limitations	I	NA	NA	NA
		II	FL 17C	FL 18NC, 19S	FL 20,
		III	NA	FL 21SC, 22SC, 23, 24	FL 25, 26
ACS I. G. ☐	Operation of Systems	I	NA	NA	NA
		II	FL 17C	FL 18NC, 19SC	FL 20
		III	NA	21SC, 22SC	NA
ACS I. H. ☐	Human Factors	I	FL 3	FL 4	FL 10
		II	NA	NA	NA
		III	NA	FL 23, 24	FL 25, 26
Part 141 Appendix B (ii) FAR 61.107 (ii) ACS II.	**Preflight Procedures**				
ACS II. A. ☐	Preflight Assessment (Self-Assessment and Preflight Inspection)	I	FL 1	FL 2	FL 10
		II	NA	NA	NA
		III	NA	FL 23, 24	FL 25, 26
ACS II. B. ☐	Flight Deck Management	I	FL 1	FL 2	FL 10
		II	FL 16N, 17C	FL 18NC, 19SC	FL 20
		III	NA	FL 21SC, 22SC, 23, 24	FL 25, 26
ACS II. C. ☐	Engine Starting	I	FL 1	FL 2, FL 9S	FL 10
		II	NA	NA	NA
		III	NA	FL 23, 24	FL 25, 26
ACS II. D. ☐	Taxiing	I	FL 1	FL 2, 7, 8, 9S	FL 10
		II	FL 16N	FL 12S	NA
		III	NA	FL 23, 24	FL 25, 26

Table continued on next page.

APPENDIX B ■ FAR Requirements

FAR/ACS	TASKS	STAGE	INTRODUCE	REVIEW	EVALUATE
ACS II. F. ☐	Before Takeoff Check **Before Takeoff Check/ Runup**	I	FL 1	FL 2, 9S	FL 10
		II	FL 16N	FL 12S	NA
		III	NA	FL 23, 24	FL 25, 26
Part 141 Appendix B (iii) FAR 61.107 (iii) ACS III.	**Airport and Seaplane Base Operations**				
ACS III. A. ☐	Communications and Light Signals **Radio Communications**	I	FL 2	FL 3, 7, 8, 9S	FL 10
		II	NA	FL 11, 12S, 13S, 17C, 18SC, 19SC	FL 20
		III	NA	FL 21S, 22S, 23, 24	FL 25, 26
ACS III. A. ☐	Light Signals **Lost Communication Procedures/ATC Light Signals**	I	FL 6	FL 7, 8	FL 10
		II	NA	NA	NA
		III	NA	FL 23, 24	FL 25, 26
ACS III. B. ☐	Traffic Patterns **Traffic Patterns/ Departure, Arrival, Entry, and Approach Procedures**	I	FL 2	FL 3, 7, 8, 9S	FL 10
		II	NA	FL 11, 12S 17C, 18NC, 19S	FL 20
		III	NA	FL 21S, 22S, 23, 24	FL 25, 26
Part 141 Appendix B (iv) FAR 61.107 (iv) ACS IV.	**Takeoffs, Landings, and Go-Arounds**				
ACS IV. A. ☐	Normal Takeoff and Climb	I	FL 1	FL 2, 3, 4, 5, 7, 8, 9S	FL 10
		II	FL 16N	FL 12S, 13S, 15, 16N	FL 20
		III	NA	FL 23, 24,	FL 25, 26
ACS IV. B. ☐	Normal Approach and Landing	I	FL 1	FL 2, 3, 4, 5, 7, 8, 9S	FL 10
		II	FL 16N	FL 12S, 13S, 15, 16N	FL 20
		III	NA	FL 23, 24,	FL 25, 26
ACS IV. C. ☐	Soft-Field Takeoff and Climb	I	NA	NA	NA
		II	FL 11	FL 14, 15, 16	FL 20
		III	NA	FL 23, 24	FL 25, 26

Table continued on next page.

Private Pilot Syllabus

FAR/ACS	TASKS	STAGE	INTRODUCE	REVIEW	EVALUATE
ACS IV. D. ☐	Soft-Field Approach and Landing	I	NA	NA	NA
		II	FL 11	FL 14, 15, 16	FL 20
		III	NA	FL 23, 24	FL 25, 26
ACS IV. E. ☐	Short-Field Takeoff and Maximum Performance Climb	I	NA	NA	NA
		II	FL 11	FL 14, 15, 16	FL 20
		III	NA	FL 23, 24	FL 25, 26
ACS IV. F. ☐	Short-Field Approach and Landing	I	NA	NA	NA
		II	FL 11	FL 14, 15, 16	FL 20
		III	NA	FL 23, 24	FL 25, 26
ACS IV. M. ☐	Forward Slip to a Landing	I	FL 6	FL 7, 8	FL 10
		II	NA	NA	NA
		III	NA	FL 23, 24	FL 25, 26
ACS IV. N. ☐	Go-Around/Rejected Landing	I	FL 6	FL 7, 8, 9S	FL 10
		II	FL 16N	NA	NA
		III	NA	FL 23, 24	FL 25, 26
Part 141 Appendix B (v) (vi) **FAR 61.107 (v) (vi)** **ACS V.**	**Performance and Ground Reference Maneuvers**				
ACS V. A. ☐	Steep Turns	I	FL 4	FL 5, 7	NA
		II	FL 16N	NA	NA
		III	NA	FL 23, 24	FL 25, 26
ACS V. B. ☐	Ground Reference Maneuvers	I	FL 5	FL 6, 7	FL 10
		II	NA	FL 13S	NA
		III	NA	FL 23, 24	FL 25, 26

Table continued on next page.

APPENDIX B ■ FAR Requirements

FAR/ACS	TASKS	STAGE	INTRODUCE	REVIEW	EVALUATE
Part 141 Appendix B (vii) **FAR 61.107 (vii)** **ACS VI.**	**Navigation**				
ACS VI. A. ☐	Pilotage and Dead Reckoning	NA	NA	NA	NA
		FL 17C	FL 18NC, 19S,	FL 20	FL 20
		NA	FL 21S, 22S, 23, 24	FL 25, 26	FL 25, 26
ACS VI. B ☐	Navigation Systems and Radar Services **VOR Navigation** **GPS Navigation** **ADF Navigation, based on aircraft equipment**	I	NA	NA	NA
		II	FL 14, 17C, 18NC	FL 15, 19SC	FL 20
		III	NA	FL 21SC, 22SC, 23, 24	FL 25, 26
ACS VI. C. ☐	Diversion	I	NA	NA	NA
		II	FL 17C	FL 18NC	FL 20
		III	NA	FL 23, 24	FL 25, 26
ACS VI. D. ☐	Lost Procedures	I	NA	NA	NA
		II	FL 17C	FL 18NC	FL 20
		III	NA	FL 23, 24	FL 25, 26
Part 141 Appendix B (viii) **FAR 61.107 (viii)** **ACS VII.**	**Slow Flight and Stalls**				
ACS VII. A. ☐	Maneuvering During Slow Flight	I	FL 3	FL 4, 5, 7	FL 10
		II	FL 16N	FL 13S	NA
		III	NA	FL 23, 24	FL 25, 26
ACS VII. B. ☐	Power-Off Stalls	I	FL 3	FL 4, 5, 7	FL 10
		II	FL 16N	FL 13S	NA
		III	NA	FL 23, 24	FL 25, 26
ACS VII. C. ☐	Power-On Stalls	I	FL 3	FL 4, 5, 7	FL 10
		II	FL 16N	FL 13S	NA
		III	NA	FL 23, 24	FL 25, 26
ACS VII. D. ☐	Spin Awareness	I	FL 4	FL 5, 7	FL 10
		II	FL 16N	NA	NA
		III	NA	FL 23, 24	FL 25, 26

Table continued on next page.

Private Pilot Syllabus

FAR/ACS	TASKS	STAGE	INTRODUCE	REVIEW	EVALUATE
Part 141 Appendix B (ix) **FAR 61.107 (ix)** **ACS VIII.**	**Basic Instrument Maneuvers**				
ACS VIII. A. ☐	Straight-and-Level Flight	I	FL 3	FL 4, 5, 7	NA
		II	NA	NA	NA
		III	NA	FL 23, 24	FL 24, 25
ACS VIII. B. ☐	Constant Airspeed Climbs	I	FL 3	FL 4, 5, 7	NA
		II	NA	NA	NA
		III	NA	FL 23, 24	FL 24, 25
ACS VIII. C. ☐	Constant Airspeed Descents	I	FL 3	FL 4, 5, 7	NA
		II	NA	NA	NA
		III	NA	FL 23, 24	FL 24, 25
ACS VIII. D. ☐	Turns to Headings	I	FL 3	FL 4, 5, 7	NA
		II	NA	NA	NA
		III	NA	FL 23, 24	FL 24, 25
ACS VIII. E. ☐	Recovery from Unusual Flight Attitudes	I	NA	NA	NA
		II	FL 14	FL 15, 17C, 18NC	FL 20
		III	NA	FL 23, 24	FL 25, 26
ACS VIII. F. ☐	Radio Communications, navigation Systems/ Facilities, and Radar Services	I	NA	NA	NA
		II	FL 14	FL 15, 17C, 18NC	FL 20
		III	NA	FL 23, 24	FL 25, 26
Part 141 Appendix B (x) **FAR 61.107 (x)** **ACS IX.**	**Emergency Operations**				
ACS IX. A. ☐	Emergency Descent	I	FL 4	FL 5, 7	FL 10
		II	NA	FL 17, 18NC	FL 20
		III	NA	FL 23, 24	FL 25, 26

Table continued on next page.

APPENDIX B ■ FAR Requirements

FAR/ACS	TASKS	STAGE	INTRODUCE	REVIEW	EVALUATE
ACS IX. B. ☐	Emergency Approach and Landing (Simulated)	I	FL 4	FL 5, 7, 8	FL 10
		II	NA	FL 17, 18NC	FL 20
		III	NA	FL 23, 24	FL 25, 26
ACS IX. C. ☐	Systems and Equipment Malfunctions	I	FL 4	FL 5, 7, 8	FL 10
		II	NA	FL 17, 18NC	FL 20
		III	NA	FL 23, 24	FL 25, 26
ACS IX. D. ☐	Emergency Equipment and Survival Gear	I	FL 4	FL 5, 7	FL 10
		II	NA	FL 17, 18NC	FL 20
		III	NA	FL 23, 24	FL 25, 26
Part 141 Appendix B (xi) FAR 61.107 (xi) ACS XI.	**Night Operations**				
ACS XI. A. ☐	Night Preparation / **Preflight Preparation—Night** / **Preflight Procedures—Night**	I	FL 16N	FL 18NC	NA
		II	NA	NA	NA
		III	NA	NA	NA
Part 141 Appendix B (xii) FAR 61.107 (xii) ACS XII.	**Postflight Procedures**				
ACS XII. A. ☐	After Landing, Parking, and Securing	I	FL 1	FL 2, 9S	FL 10
		II	NA	FL 12S	NA
		III	NA	FL 23, 24	FL 25, 26

This is to Certify that

_____

is enrolled in the

Federal Aviation Administration _____ course

approved _____

conducted by _____.

_____
Chief Instructor

_____
Date of Enrollment

This is to certify that

_____

has successfully completed all stages, tests, and
course requirements and has graduated from the
FEDERAL AVIATION ADMINISTRATION

approved _____ course

conducted by _____

The graduate has completed the cross-country
training specified in FAR Part 141.

☐ Private Pilot Certification Course —
    Appendix B, Paragraphs 4 and 5

☐ Instrument Rating Course — Appendix C,
    Paragraph 4(c)(1)(ii)

☐ Commercial Pilot Certification Course —
    Appendix D, Paragraphs 4 and 5

☐ Other: _____

I certify the above statements are true.

_____
Chief Instructor

_____
School certificate number

_____
Date of graduation